W9-CSM-678

[the Visual] Guide to First Grade

Grade 1

Thinking Kids™
An imprint of Carson-Dellosa Publishing LLC
P.O. Box 35665
Greensboro, NC 27425 USA

Thinking Kids™
An imprint of Carson-Dellosa Publishing LLC
P.O. Box 35665
Greensboro, NC 27425 USA

Printed in the USA • All rights reserved.
01-060167784
ISBN 978-1-4838-2682-0

Infographics and Learning Activities

BUNCHES OF BABIES

How many baby animals are in one litter?

1 BLUE WHALE

2 BLACK BEARS

6 RABBITS

7 OPOSSUMS

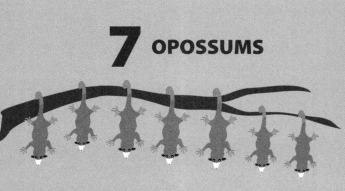

11 ARCTIC FOXES

3 SQUIRRELS

4 HEDGEHOGS

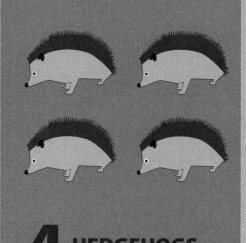

5 WILD PIGS

7 MICE

10 DUCKS

15 TENRECS

20 GARTER SNAKES

The Visual Guide to First Grade

Do the Math

2

Write a number below each picture. Solve the problems.

1. How many in three litters of black bears?

2 + 2 + 2 = 6

2. How many more in a litter of ducks?

 –  =

10 – 6 = 4

3. How many more in a litter of tenrecs?

 –  =

15 – 5 = 10

4. How many in four litters of squirrels?

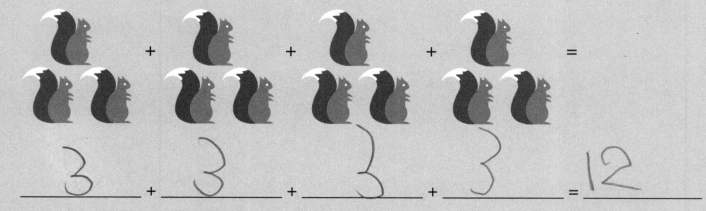

3 + 3 + 3 + 3 = 12

Describe It

Adjectives are describing words. Write an adjective from the box to complete each sentence.

| strong | tall | large | four |
| small | orange | white | bushy |

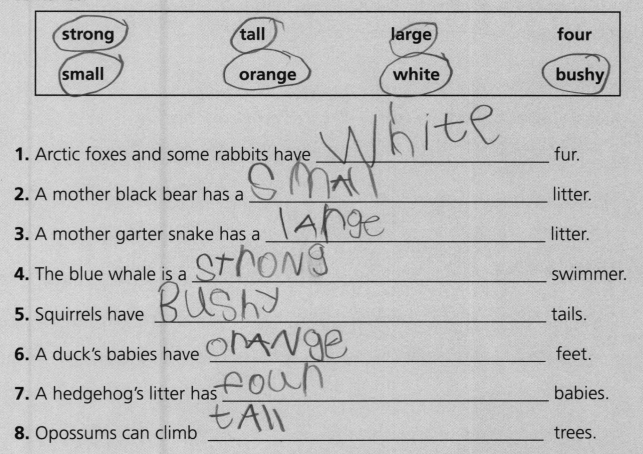

1. Arctic foxes and some rabbits have _White_ fur.

2. A mother black bear has a _Small_ litter.

3. A mother garter snake has a _large_ litter.

4. The blue whale is a _strong_ swimmer.

5. Squirrels have _Bushy_ tails.

6. A duck's babies have _orange_ feet.

7. A hedgehog's litter has _four_ babies.

8. Opossums can climb _tall_ trees.

Sun Power

The Sun is the most powerful engine we know. It makes life on Earth possible. Scientists and inventors are working on new ways to trap and use energy from the Sun.

The Sun is 93 million miles (150 million km) away from Earth. It takes light 10 minutes to get here!

The largest solar energy plant is in the desert in California.

Hang laundry on the line to dry. You are using Sun power!

Solar energy makes no pollution. It is free, and we will never run out!

Enough sunlight falls on Earth in one hour to power the world . . . for a year!

Solar panels collect the Sun's energy. That energy can be used to heat a home or power a TV.

A Solar House

Solar panels make DC* electricity from the Sun's energy.

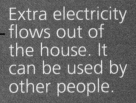

Extra electricity flows out of the house. It can be used by other people.

The inverter changes the electricity from DC to AC†.

The AC electricity flows to the outlets in the house.

*DC electricity is the kind in a battery.
†AC electricity is the kind used by a plug.

Make an Idea Web

Read the sentences. Some are true. Some are false. Write the numbers of the true sentences in the web.

1. The Sun is more than 100 million miles from Earth.

2. Solar panels make DC electricity.

3. A desert is not a good place for a solar energy plant.

4. The Sun creates energy.

5. Sunlight takes 10 minutes to get to Earth.

6. Solar panels on a roof can make more electricity than a house needs.

7. Solar energy is free, but it creates a lot of pollution.

8. A puddle dries up because of solar energy.

Try It Yourself

Use the power of the Sun to cook! Follow the steps to make your own solar oven. You will need an adult's help.

What you need:
• a box with a lid, like a pizza box
• aluminum foil
• tape or a glue stick
• plastic wrap
• a stick or ruler
• bread and butter

What you do:

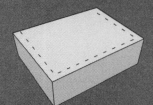

1. Have an adult cut out most of the lid of the box.

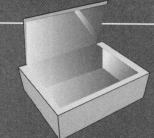

2. Use tape or a glue stick to attach aluminum foil. Cover the inside of the cutout lid with foil. Cover the inside of the box with foil. Make sure the foil is flat and smooth.

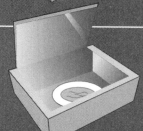

3. Butter some bread. Set it inside the box on the aluminum foil.

4. Tape two layers of plastic wrap across the opening in the box. For the first layer, put the tape under the edge of the opening. For the second layer, put the tape on top of the opening. Now you have a plastic window. It will keep in the heat.

5. Use a stick or ruler to prop up the lid. Set the oven in the sunlight. Wait for about half an hour.

What happened to the bread? Write about it.

_____

_____

A Trip to Ancient Egypt

Egypt is a country in Africa. Thousands of years ago, Egypt was ruled by kings called *pharaohs*. What was it like in Ancient Egypt?

Egypt

Africa

When a pharaoh died, he was often buried in a pyramid. The biggest Egyptian pyramid is the Great Pyramid of Giza. It is taller than the Statue of Liberty!

Near the Great Pyramid is the Sphinx. It is a huge statue. The Sphinx has the head of a man and the body of a lion.

Cats were special animals in Ancient Egypt. People believed having a cat was good luck.

King Tut was a young pharaoh. He died when he was only 19 years old. His tomb was found in 1922. It was filled with treasures.

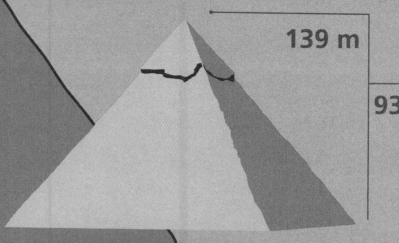

139 m

93 m

Great Pyramid of Giza

Statue of Liberty

A mummy is a body that has been made to last forever. Mummies are wrapped in long pieces of cloth. Some animals were even made into mummies!

Great Pyramid and Sphinx

Egypt

The Nile River flows through Egypt. It was an important part of life in Ancient Egypt.

The alphabet used pictures, not letters.

Think and Solve

Study the infographic. Answer the questions.

1. Animals were sometimes made into mummies.

   (True)   **False**

2. Why were cats important in Ancient Egypt?
   A. They were thought to bring good luck.
   B. They were used for hunting.
   C. They were used for food.
   D. They helped protect children.

3. Egypt is a country in _____Good luck_____.

4. Kings in Ancient Egypt were called ___pharaoh___.
   A. niles
   B. (pharaohs)
   C. sphinxes
   D. tuts

Label It

What does each picture show? Write the name on the line.

1.  _____Sphinxes_____

2.  _____pyramid_____

3.  _____mummy_____

4.  _____Tut_____

Piece It Together

The Ancient Egyptians wrote with pictures called *hieroglyphics*. You will use the hieroglyphics below to write your name or a message. Cut out the symbols you will need. Then, glue or tape them on page 19.

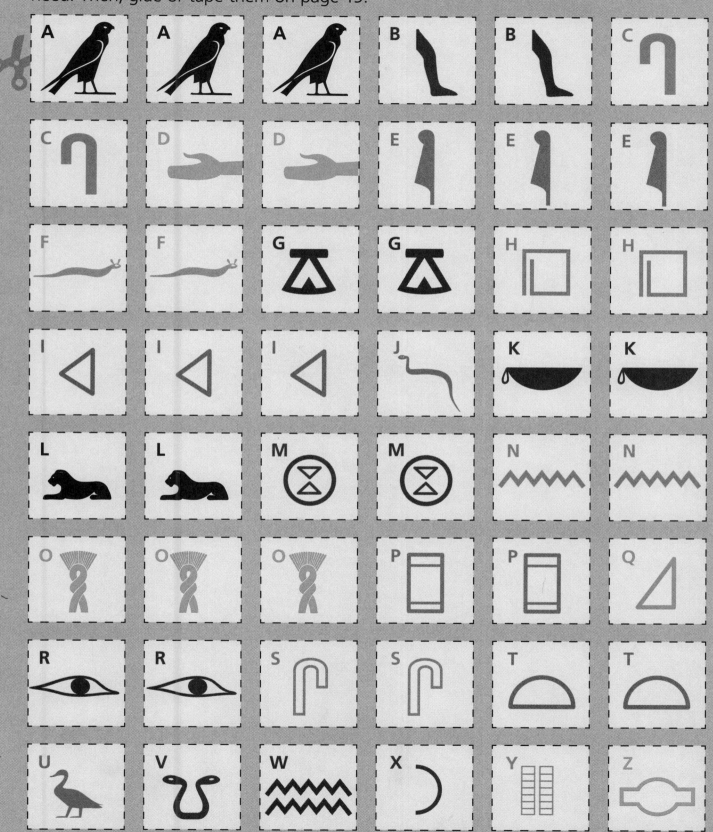

Hieroglyphics

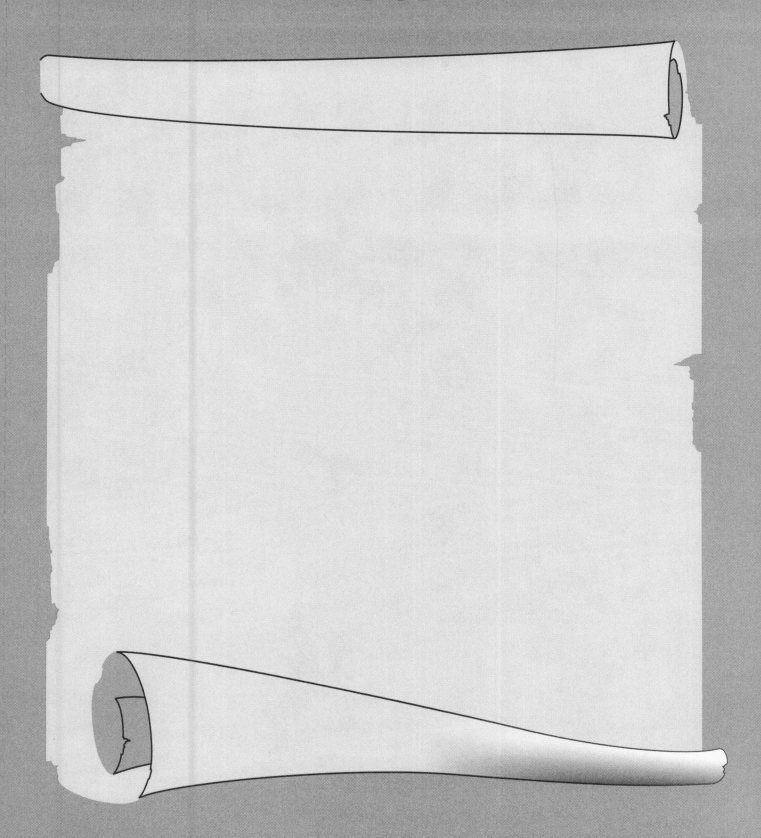

Frogs and Toads

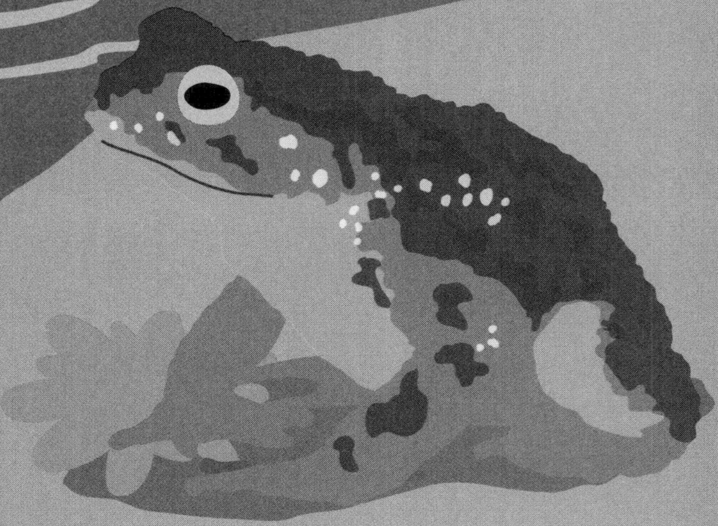

Frogs

- wet and smooth skin
- green or bright colors
- thinner body
- longer legs
- jump most of the time
- live in the water

Toads

- dry and bumpy skin
- brown
- stout body
- shorter legs
- walk most of the time
- live on land

Both

- lay eggs in water
- hatch as tadpoles in water
- eat insects
- are frogs! A toad is a type of frog.

Think and Solve

Study the infographic. Answer the questions.

1. Write a check mark on the line if the words describe both frogs and toads.

_____✗_____ green skin   _____✗_____ have long legs

_____✗_____ bumpy skin   _____✓_____ hatch as tadpoles

_____✓_____ lay eggs   _____✓_____ eat insects

2. All toads are frogs.

(True)   **False**

3. A _____ ToAd _____ walks most of the time.

Read About It: Frog or Toad?

SPLASH! LONG LEGS KICK. A smooth body swims. A green head pokes up from the water. Big eyes watch a buzzing bug go by. Zip! A quick tongue shoots out. The insect is gone.

Who ate the bug? Circle your answer.

a toad   (**a frog**)

Zooming Through History

1884
First electric car
It ran on a battery!

1769
First steam car
The first steam car had 3 wheels and could only go a little more than 2 miles per hour!

1948
First drive–through

1940
First car with air conditioning

1949
First VW Beetles sold in the US

1960
Gas cost 31 cents a gallon

1965
Most cars had front seat belts

1976
Cars from Japan were popular

2015
A new car cost about $30,000 dollars!

2010
Gas cost $2.73 a gallon

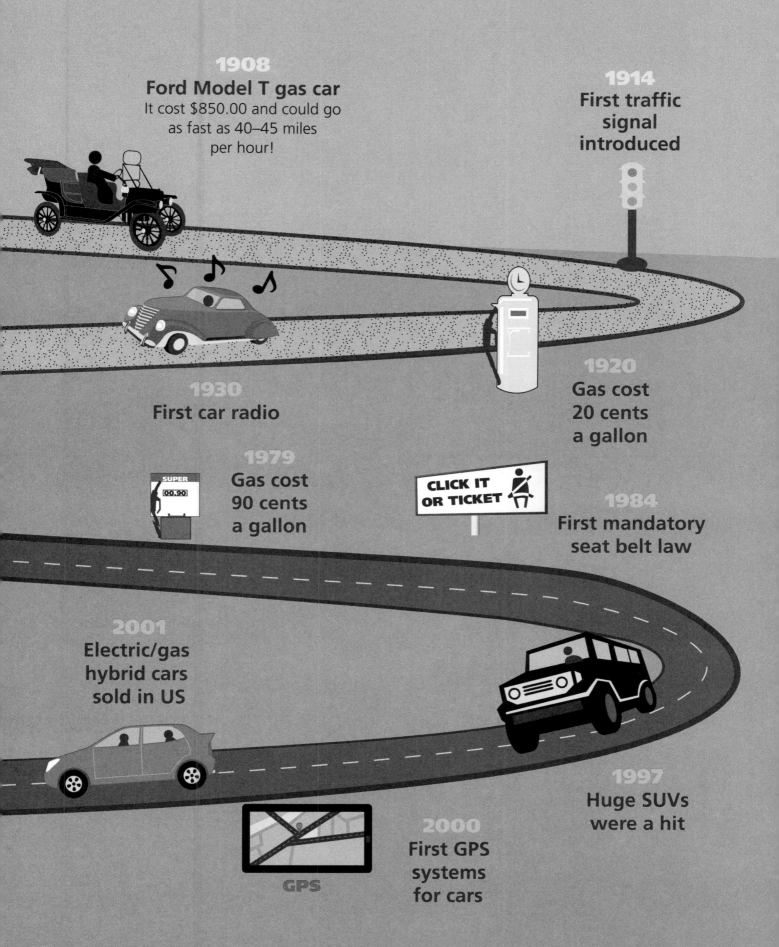

1908
Ford Model T gas car
It cost $850.00 and could go
as fast as 40–45 miles
per hour!

1914
**First traffic
signal
introduced**

1930
First car radio

1920
**Gas cost
20 cents
a gallon**

1979
**Gas cost
90 cents
a gallon**

SUPER
00.90

CLICK IT
OR TICKET

1984
**First mandatory
seat belt law**

2001
**Electric/gas
hybrid cars
sold in US**

1997
**Huge SUVs
were a hit**

GPS

2000
**First GPS
systems
for cars**

Think and Solve

Study the infographic. Answer the questions.

1. The first cars used steam for power.

True   **False**

2. Gas cost _____ cents a gallon in 1920.

3. What came before the first car radio?
   A. the first traffic signal
   B. the first VW Beetle
   C. most cars have seat belts
   D. the first drive-through

Label It

Read each statement. Write the year in which the person might have said it. Use the infographic to help you.

My gallon of gas costs 90 cents.

_____

I want to drive an SUV.

_____

My horseless carriage is electric.

_____

I bought a Model T for $850.

_____

This new seat belt will keep me safe.

_____

Explore Your World

Choose a gas station you see often. Then, choose a day of the week. On that day each week, notice the price for a gallon of gas. Record it below.

WEEK 1

REGULAR GAS

$ _____

WEEK 2

REGULAR GAS

$ _____

WEEK 3

REGULAR GAS

$ _____

WEEK 4

REGULAR GAS

$ _____

Now, use the prices you wrote to answer the questions. Circle or write your answers.

From Week 1 to Week 2, the price went (up, down).

From Week 2 to Week 3, the price went (up, down).

From Week 3 to Week 4, the price went (up, down).

Compare the prices for Week 1 and Week 4. How did the price change?

The price went (up, down) by _____cents.

All About Bikes

Using pedal power is a great way to travel. Bike riding is fast and fun. It is good for you and for our planet.

Parts of a Bike

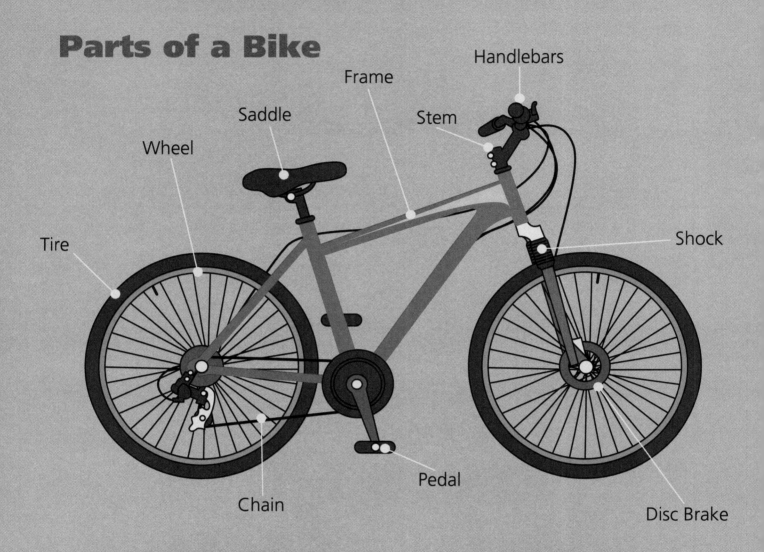

Frame

Handlebars

Saddle

Stem

Wheel

Shock

Tire

Pedal

Chain

Disc Brake

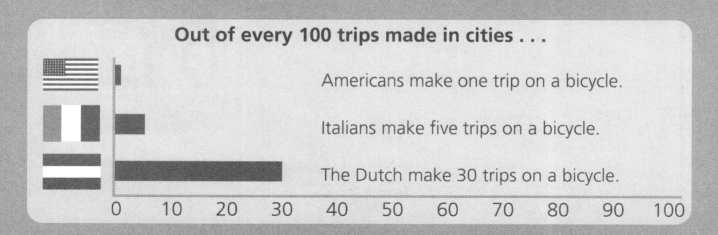

Out of every 100 trips made in cities . . .

Americans make one trip on a bicycle.

Italians make five trips on a bicycle.

The Dutch make 30 trips on a bicycle.

0   10   20   30   40   50   60   70   80   90   100

Did you know . . .

There are about 1 billion bikes in the world.

The longest bike ever made seated 35 people.

You can park about 15 bicycles in the same space that one car takes.

The Tour de France is the most famous bicycle race.

The Wright brothers owned a bike shop. They built the first airplane there.

Fred Birchmore rode his bike around the world in 1935.

Bikes were first called *velocipedes*.

100 million bikes are made each year.

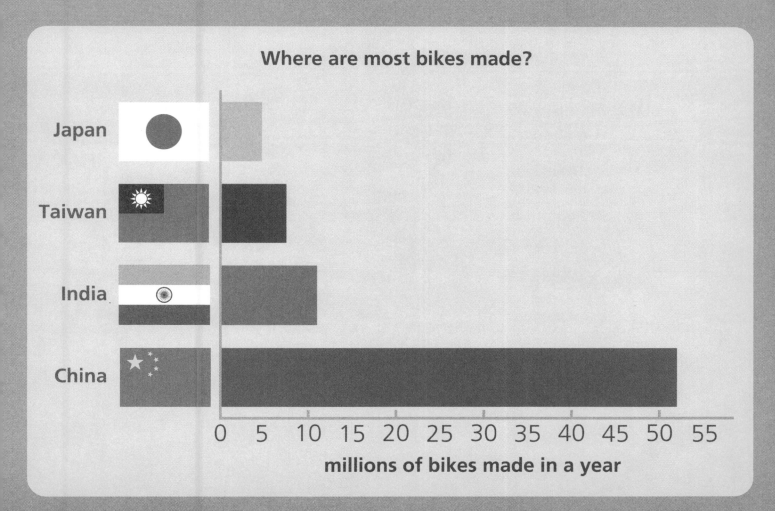

Where are most bikes made?

millions of bikes made in a year

Think and Solve

Study the infographic. Answer the questions.

1. Most bikes are made _____.

    A. in the US

    B. by the Dutch

    C. in China

    D. in Japan

2. The seat of a bike is called a *saddle*.

    True   **False**

3. There are about one _____ bikes in the world.

Do the Math

Solve the problems. Use the infographic to help you.

1. Out of 100 trips, how many more do the Dutch make on bicycles than Italians?

_____ trips

2. How many bikes can fit into two parking spaces for cars?

_____ bikes

3. Japan makes 5 million bikes each year. India makes 11 million bikes each year. How many more bikes does India make each year?

_____ million

Label It

The prefix *uni-* means "one."   The prefix *bi-* means "two."

The prefix *tri-* means "three."   The word part *cycle* means "circle."

Label each picture with a word from the box.

tricycle	unicycle	motorcycle	bicycle

_____   _____

_____   _____

Puzzle It

Look for the names of bike parts in the puzzle. Circle each word.

I	K	N	W	T	F	X	P	N	G	D	G
R	O	G	A	S	E	M	A	R	F	N	N
X	O	B	M	A	C	K	J	S	I	B	Q
T	I	R	E	D	L	K	C	A	T	E	Q
C	N	O	C	D	A	M	H	O	B	E	D
S	W	K	U	L	D	C	R	K	H	Z	M
S	H	S	M	E	E	A	W	C	J	S	X
D	B	Z	S	V	P	H	R	Z	I	F	Y
F	W	I	S	X	E	A	L	F	D	F	J
Z	E	F	G	E	X	H	U	F	K	U	M
T	G	H	L	B	W	G	F	W	B	H	O
L	U	W	W	R	Y	K	Q	S	C	F	P

tire

wheel

saddle

frame

stem

shock

pedal

chain

The World Above

Look up. Is the sky light or dark? You will see different things in the sky during the day and during the night.

CLOUDS
are made up of tiny drops of water.

PLANES

THE SUN
is about 93 million miles from Earth. There would be no life on Earth without it.

RAINBOWS
happen when sunlight hits raindrops. The water separates the light into bands of color.

RAINDROPS
fall when lots of droplets collect in clouds. The drops get bigger and heavier. Gravity pulls them to the ground.

HOT-AIR BALLOONS
float because the hot air inside the balloon is less dense than the cooler air outside.

BIRDS

DAY

The Visual Guide to First Grade

THE INTERNATIONAL SPACE STATION (ISS)

can be seen from Earth. Go online to find out when it will pass over you!

SHOOTING STARS

are not really stars. They are meteors. They are very hot but burn up quickly.

STARS

are easier to see away from city lights.

VENUS

looks like a very bright star. You can see it right after sunset or before sunrise.

PLANES

New Moon

THE MOON

is about 250,000 miles away from Earth. It travels around Earth once about every 29 days.

MOONBOWS

are night rainbows. They are made with moonlight and drops of water.

BATS

are animals of the night. They hunt bugs at night and stay safe from predators.

NIGHT

Think and Solve

Study the infographic. Answer the questions.

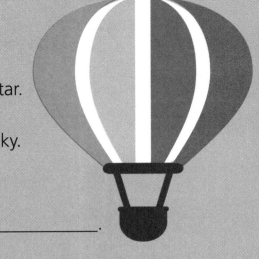

1. The planet _____ looks like a bright star.

2. Shooting stars are stars that move quickly across the sky.

    True   **False**

3. A rainbow that happens at night is called a _____.

4. What are clouds made of?

_____

Color It

Read each fact. If it tells about something in the day, color the windows blue. If it tells about something in the night, color the windows yellow.

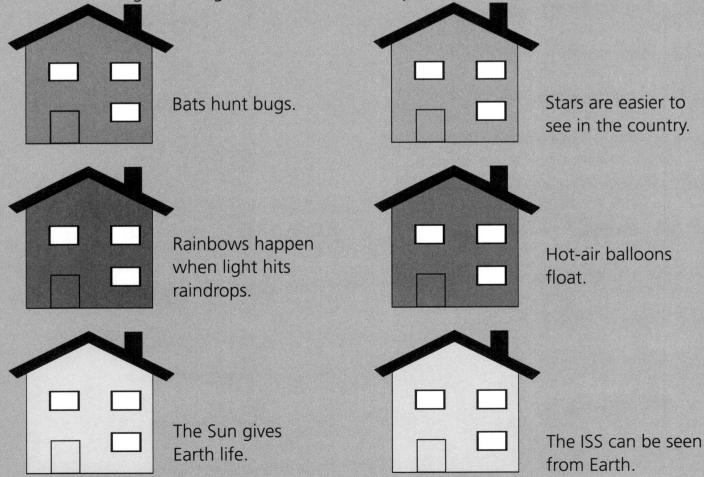

Bats hunt bugs.

Stars are easier to see in the country.

Rainbows happen when light hits raindrops.

Hot-air balloons float.

The Sun gives Earth life.

The ISS can be seen from Earth.

Piece It Together

Cut apart the pictures that show what Mateo does during one day. Then, glue or tape each picture onto page 35. Be sure the pictures are in time order and in the right part of the day. Use the time next to each picture and the clock faces as hints.

morning

afternoon

evening

night

Long, Longer, Longest!

Animals come in all shapes and sizes. Some are long.
Some are much longer!

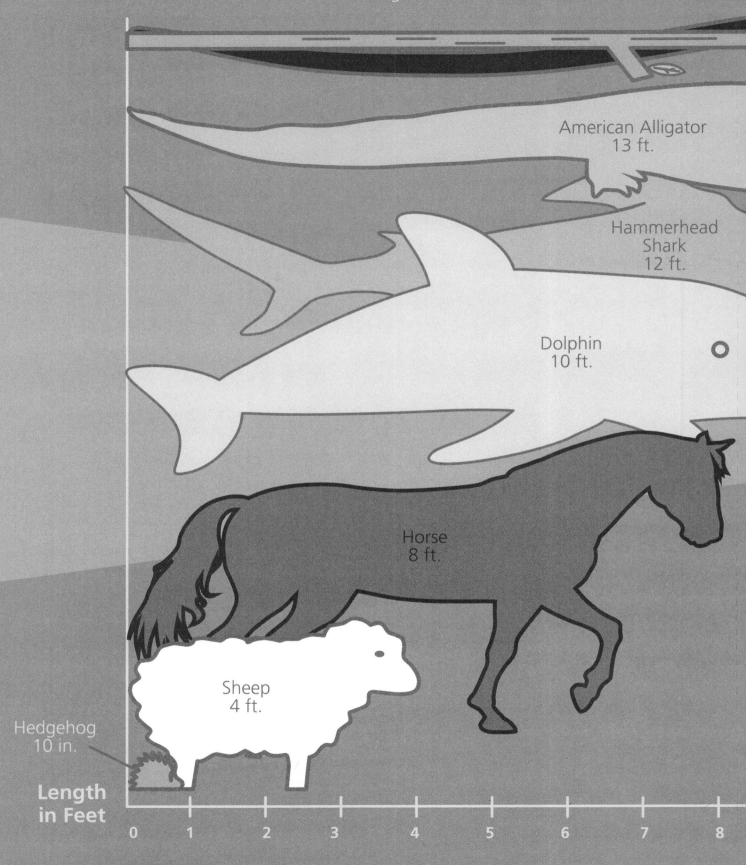

American Alligator
13 ft.

Hammerhead
Shark
12 ft.

Dolphin
10 ft.

Horse
8 ft.

Sheep
4 ft.

Hedgehog
10 in.

**Length
in Feet**

0   1   2   3   4   5   6   7   8

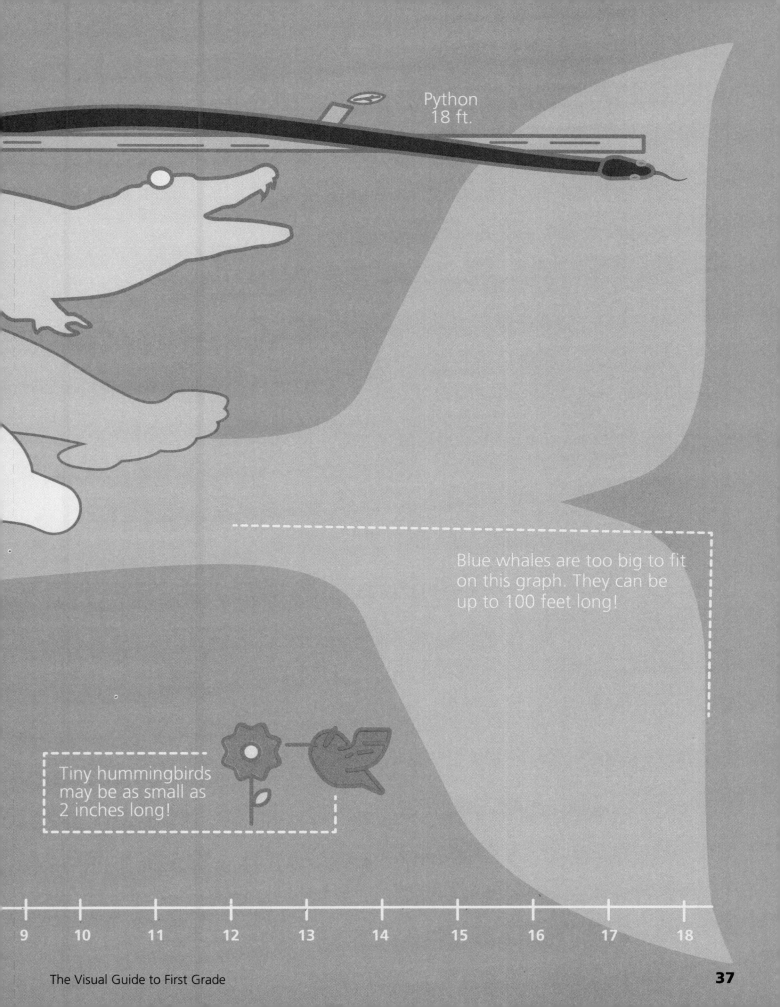

Python
18 ft.

Blue whales are too big to fit on this graph. They can be up to 100 feet long!

Tiny hummingbirds may be as small as 2 inches long!

9 10 11 12 13 14 15 16 17 18

Think and Solve

Study the infographic. Answer the questions.

1. How long is a dolphin?
   A. 9 feet
   B. 10 feet
   C. 11 feet
   D. 12 feet

2. A foot is 12 inches. A hedgehog is (shorter, longer) than one foot.

   Shorter

3. The longest animal in the infographic is the python.
   (True)   False

Do the Math

Solve the problems. Use the infographic to help you.

1. An American alligator is __5__ feet longer than a horse.

2. A dolphin is __2__ feet shorter than a hammerhead shark.

3. Four sheep stand in a row. Is the row of sheep longer or shorter than a python?

   shorter

Try It Yourself

How long are you? Lie on the floor. Have a friend use a tape measure to measure you from the bottom of your feet to the top of your head. Write your height below.

_____ feet and _____ inches

Measure It

Look inside and outside. Find four small things to measure. Make sure each one is less than eight inches long. Use a ruler to measure each thing. Then, draw it on the chart to show its length.

American Indian Homes

Native American tribes built many different types of homes.

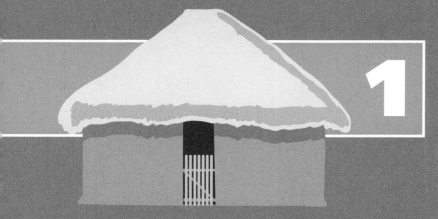

1

Wattle and Daub Hut
- built by tribes in the Southeast, like the Cherokee
- the shape was made from thick grasses and vines covered with daub (a kind of mud)
- the roof was made of grass or wood shingles

2

Adobe Pueblo
- used by the Pueblo people of the Southwest
- made from stone or adobe (clay) bricks
- stair-step design, up to five stories tall
- many families could live in one building

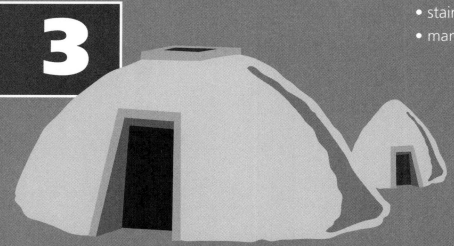

3

Hogan
- built by the Navajo Indians of the Southwest
- shaped like a dome and covered by mud or grass
- had a chimney and no windows

4

Tepee
- used by Plains Indians
- usually made of buffalo skins stretched on wooden poles

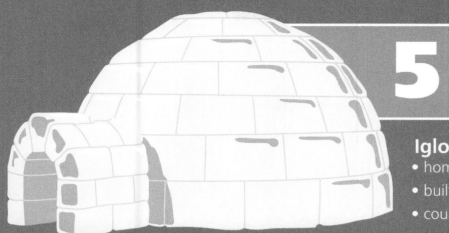

5

Igloo
- home to the Inuit of the Arctic
- built with snow blocks
- could be made in just a few hours

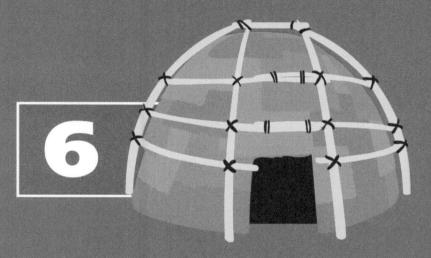

6

Wickiup
- also called a *wigwam*
- used mostly by tribes in the Northeast
- made by bending thin, young trees and tying them together
- the trees were covered with woven grasses or bark

7

Longhouse
- used mostly by tribes in the Northeast
- made by bending thin, young trees and tying them together
- covered with bark or wood shingles
- 40 to 400 feet long

Think and Solve
Study the infographic. Answer the questions.

1. Which type of home has the same shape as an igloo?
   A. tepee
   B. wickiup
   C. longhouse
   D. pueblo

2. Pueblos were used by people in the _____ part of the US.

3. Which two types of houses were used in the Northeast?

_____ and _____

Match It
Draw a line to match each home with its description.

Wattle and Daub Hut

built by the Navajo

Hogan

up to 400 feet long

Longhouse

also called a *wigwam*

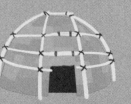
Wickiup

roof made of grass

Make a Chart

Check what was used to make each house. The first one is done for you.

Type of House	grass	mud	brick	wood	animal skins	snow
	✓	✓		✓		

Write About It

Which house would you like to live in? Why?

_____

_____

_____

The Dirt on Dirt

What's going on beneath your feet? A lot!
Earth's soil is made up of different layers.

O Top Layer

This layer has dead leaves, grass, and living insects.
It is sometimes called the *litter layer*.

A
Topsoil

This layer is made up of sand, fine dirt,
minerals, water, and air. There may be small
stones or pebbles. Seeds sprout and roots
grow in the topsoil. Many insects and
bacteria live in the topsoil, too.

Bacteria

B
Subsoil

This layer is made of harder dirt and bigger rocks.
The roots of trees and big plants grow in the
subsoil. Very few bugs live here.

C
Regolith

This layer is mostly rock. Roots do not reach this
deep. There are no living plants or animals.

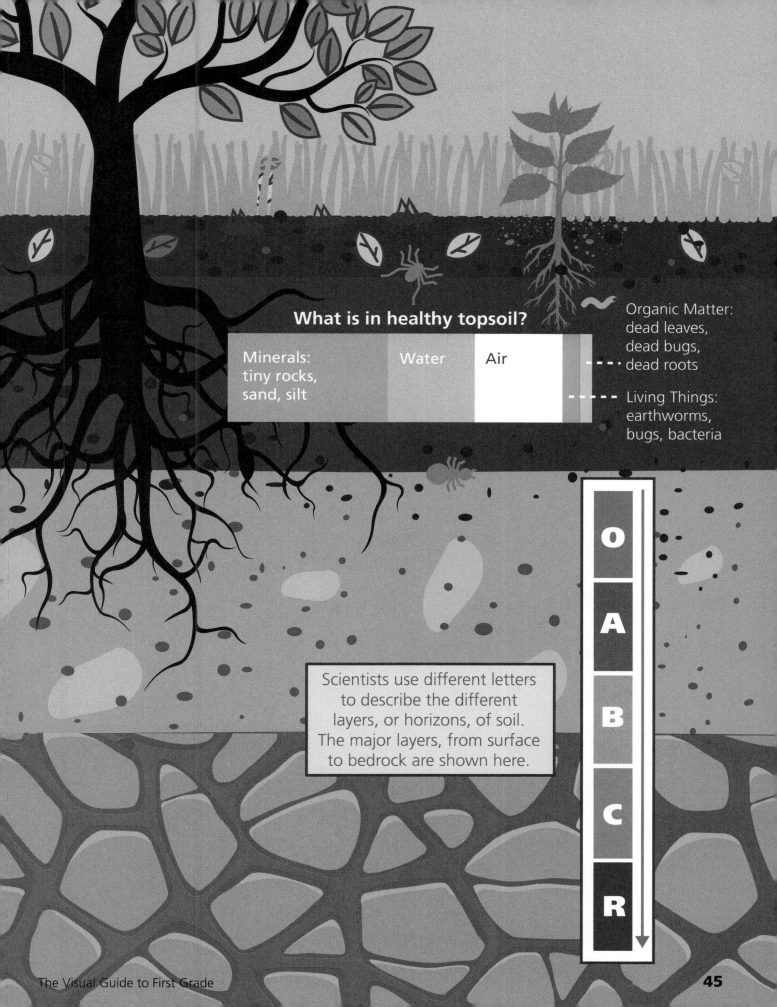

What is in healthy topsoil?

Minerals: tiny rocks, sand, silt

Water

Air

Organic Matter: dead leaves, dead bugs, dead roots

Living Things: earthworms, bugs, bacteria

Scientists use different letters to describe the different layers, or horizons, of soil. The major layers, from surface to bedrock are shown here.

O
A
B
C
R

Think and Solve

Study the infographic. Answer the questions.

1. Healthy topsoil is mostly water.

True   **False**

2. In which layers do roots grow?
   A. O and A
   B. B and C
   C. A and B
   D. A and C

3. A mole digs tunnels underground. It is looking for insects to eat. Which soil layer does the mole dig in?

_____

4. Layer R is the lowest layer. It is called *bedrock*. Tell what you think Layer R is like.

_____

_____

Identify It

Read each statement. Write the letter of the soil layer that is being described.

_____ This layer has the roots of big trees.

_____ This layer has lots of bugs and grass.

_____ This layer has no living things.

_____ This layer is where seeds grow.

Piece It Together

Cut apart the pictures of things that are found underground. Glue or tape each picture in the correct soil layer on page 49.

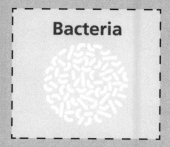

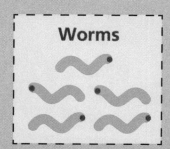

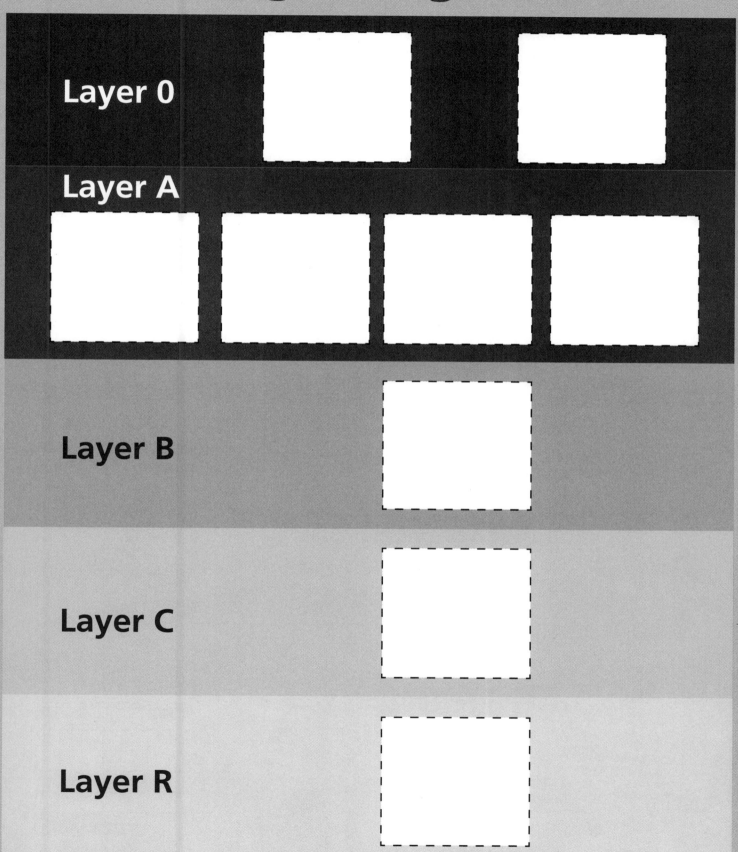

Layer 0

Layer A

Layer B

Layer C

Layer R

Becoming the President

Would you like to be the president of the United States someday?
Here is what you need to do.

First

You need experience. You should work in the government.

What did presidents do before they became president?

12 were generals in the Army

35 were members of Congress

17 were state governors

Next

You need to meet three requirements.

1. Were you a US citizen when you were born?

Yes ↓   No →

2. Have you lived in the US for at least 14 years?

Yes ↓   No →

3. Are you at least 35 years old?

Yes ↓   No →

Yes. You can run for president!

You cannot be president.

Last

You need to get the most votes. Every 4 years, Americans vote for the president.

Election Day is in November. It is on the Tuesday after the first Monday.

If you win, you become the new president on January 20.

NOVEMBER

S	M	T	W	Th	F	S
		1	2	3	4	5
6	7	★8	9	10	11	12
13	14	15	16	17	18	19
20	21	22	23	24	25	26
27	28	29	30			

DECEMBER

S	M	T	W	Th	F	S
				1	2	3
4	5	6	7	8	9	10
11	12	13	14	15	16	17
18	19	20	21	22	23	24
25	26	27	28	29	30	31

JANUARY

S	M	T	W	Th	F	S
1	2	3	4	5	6	7
8	9	10	11	12	13	14
15	16	17	18	19	20★	21
22	23	24	25	26	27	28
29	30	31				

Think and Solve

Study the infographic. Answer the questions.

The White House

1. Most presidents were state governors before becoming president.

   True   **False**

2. A person becomes the new president about one month after being elected.

   True   **False**

3. Which is not a requirement for becoming president?

   A. You must be at least 35 years old.

   B. You must be born a US citizen.

   C. You must serve in the US Congress.

   D. You must have lived in the US for at least 14 years.

4. Read about each person. Circle **Yes** if he or she can become president.
   Circle **No** if he or she cannot become president.

   Mia is 55 years old. She was born in Miami, Florida. She has lived in the US her whole life.

   Yes   **No**

   Jonas is 64 years old. He was born in London, England. He came to the US when he was 14 years old. He became a US citizen when he was 22 years old.

   Yes   **No**

   Nancy is 37 years old. She was born in Japan, but she was a US citizen when she was born. She moved back to the US when she was 20.

   Yes   **No**

SEE YOU IN SPRING!

The leaves fall off the trees. The weather gets colder. Nature is going to sleep.
It is a tough time to find food. Many animals hibernate to survive the winter.

WHAT IS HIBERNATION?

Some animals go into a very deep sleep in winter. They make a den or burrow under the ground or into a hollow log. Their body temperature drops. They breathe more slowly. Some wake up a few times to eat. Others sleep all winter.

Black bears can gain 30 pounds a week before they hibernate.

Snakes hibernate in burrows. Sometimes, they come out in the sun to warm up.

Frogs and turtles burrow into mud at the bottom of ponds.

skunks

toads

snails

raccoons

WHO ELSE HIBERNATES?

ZZZZZZZZZZZZZZZZZZZ!

Some bats hibernate in clumps in hollow trees.

Even queen bees can hibernate!

Tree squirrels do not actually hibernate. But, they do sleep a lot in the winter. High in trees inside nests called *dreys*, they get cozy in groups to stay warm.

Groundhogs are also called *woodchucks*. A groundhog's heart beats very slowly when it hibernates.

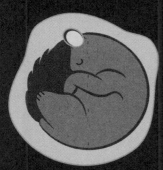

Chipmunks wake up to eat food every few days. Then, they go back to sleep.

Think and Solve

Study the infographic. Answer the questions.

1. Why do you think some animals gain weight before they hibernate?

_____

2. Squirrels sleep a lot in winter, but they do not hibernate.

True　　　　　**False**

3. Why do snakes sometimes come out of their burrows in winter?

   A. to eat

   B. to get warm

   C. to exercise

   D. to get fresh air

Identify It

Write the name of an animal to answer each question.

1. Who sleeps in the mud of a pond?_____

2. Who sleeps inside a tree trunk? _____

3. Who wakes up to eat every few days? _____

4. Who gains a lot of weight before sleeping? _____

5. Who is an insect that hibernates? _____

Read About It:
The Poorwill and the Ladybug

THE POORWILL IS AN UNUSUAL BIRD. It is one of the only birds to hibernate! The poorwill eats insects. When the weather is too cold for insects to live, the poorwill has no food. It will find a hollow log or a patch of grass to sleep in. When the weather gets warm again, the poorwill wakes up.

Another unusual hibernator is the ladybug. In winter, ladybugs huddle together in huge groups. Being together helps them to stay warm. They gather by the hundreds under leaves or bark.

Show It

It is winter in the forest. Draw a poorwill hibernating. Draw a group of ladybugs keeping warm.

Many think that Jackie Joyner-Kersee is the best female athlete of all time. She could run fast, jump high, and throw far. Jackie also has asthma. But she never let it slow her down.

Jackie Joyner-Kersee

Best Shot Put: 16 meters

Best High Jump: 2 meters

Best Javelin Throw: 50 meters

Best 800 meter run: 2 minutes, $8\frac{1}{2}$ seconds

Best 200 meter run: $22\frac{1}{2}$ seconds

Best Heptathlon Score: 7,291 points

Jackie set an Olympic record for the women's long jump. In 1988, she jumped almost $7\frac{1}{2}$ meters. That's about as long as $1\frac{1}{2}$ cars!

$7\frac{1}{2}$ meters

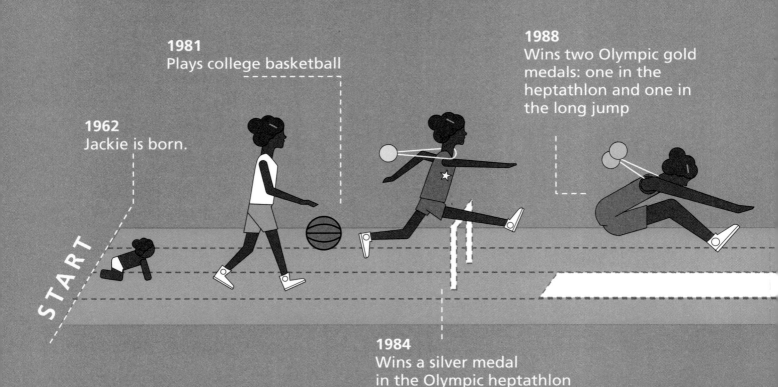

1981
Plays college basketball

1988
Wins two Olympic gold medals: one in the heptathlon and one in the long jump

1962
Jackie is born.

START

1984
Wins a silver medal in the Olympic heptathlon

A *shot* is a heavy metal ball. It weighs about the same as a gallon of milk. Jackie could throw the shot 16 meters! That's about as long as a semi truck trailer.

16 meters

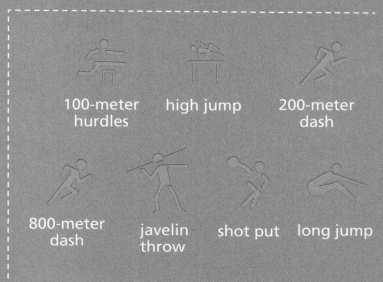

100-meter hurdles

high jump

200-meter dash

800-meter dash

javelin throw

shot put

long jump

The heptathlon has seven events. An athlete scores points for each event. Jackie Joyner-Kersee has the world record for the most points scored in a heptathlon.

1992
Wins an Olympic gold medal in the heptathlon and a bronze medal in the long jump

1996
Wins an Olympic bronze medal in the long jump

FINISH

1998
Jackie retires from sports.

Study the infographic. Answer the questions.

1. Jackie Joyner-Kersee won medals at _____ different Summer Olympics.

2. How many Olympic medals did Jackie Joyner-Kersee win?

_____ gold medals _____ silver medals _____ bronze medals

3. Jackie holds the world record for the highest score in the heptathlon.

True   **False**

4. Jackie Joyner-Kersee has _____.
   A. diabetes
   B. asthma
   C. arthritis
   D. hearing loss

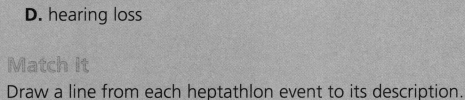

Match It

Draw a line from each heptathlon event to its description.

high jump over a bar

100-meter race with jumping

200-meter race

throwing a heavy metal ball

jumping far

throwing a long spear

800-meter race

Host your own heptathlon! Choose seven events. Then, compete with your friends. Some ideas for events are shown below. Make a check mark beside events you will use. Write your own ideas on the blank lines.

Jumping

☐ Jump the farthest.

☐ Jump the highest.

☐ Hop on one foot the longest.

☐ Jump with a cup of water without spilling.

☐ _____

Throwing

☐ Throw a ball the farthest.

☐ Throw a Frisbee the farthest.

☐ Throw a feather the farthest.

☐ Throw a ball through a hole.

☐ _____

Racing

☐ Run a short race.

☐ Run backward along a course.

☐ _____

☐ Run a long race.

☐ Hop along a course.

☐ _____

Write your events in the chart. Give points for first, second, and third place. If an event is hard, it should be worth more points. Write the names of the winners. Finally, count the points for each athlete. Make gold, silver, and bronze medals from paper and ribbon. Award them at the end of your heptathlon!

Events	Points			Winner		
	1st	2nd	3rd	1st	2nd	3rd

What's for Lunch?

What do you eat for lunch? Here are some school lunches from around the world.

USA

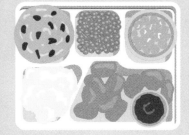

- chicken nuggets
- peas
- mashed potatoes
- fruit cocktail
- cookie

ITALY

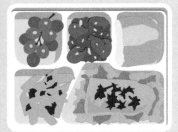

- fish and greens
- bread
- pasta
- salad
- grapes

SOUTH KOREA

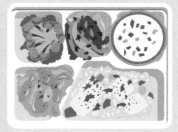

- fish soup
- tofu and rice
- veggies (pickled and fresh)

RUSSIA

- beef borscht soup
- bread
- meat
- fruit compote

BRAZIL

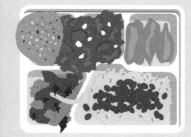

- pork
- veggies
- rice
- beans
- salad
- bread
- plantains (like bananas)

ISRAEL

- pita bread
- salad
- yogurt dip
- falafel patties (made from ground-up chickpeas)

Piece It Together

Yum! Look at all these delicious foods. Make a great meal by picking five foods from around the world. Cut out your choices. Glue or tape them onto the tray on page 63.

bratwurst
Germany

sushi
Japan

hamburger
USA

fried plantains
Brazil

spaghetti and meatballs
Italy

falafel patties
Israel

chicken dumplings
China

tamales
Mexico

crêpes
France

gyro
Greece

couscous
Morocco

chana masala
India

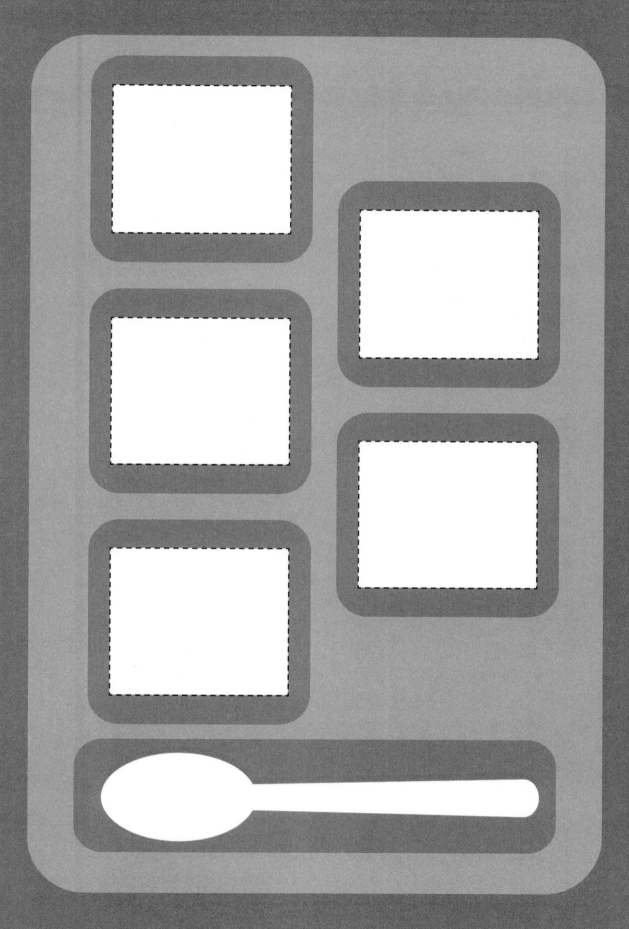

Join the Clean-Up Crew!

Earth is our home. We need to take care of it. When we pollute Earth, we make our home unsafe. How can you help keep our home clean?

Air
Smoke, dirt, and gases make the air dirty. Polluted air can cause breathing problems, like asthma.

Kinds of Pollution

Water
Polluted water is dangerous to drink. It can also make fish and other animals sick.

Land
Litter is ugly. Dangerous garbage can poison the soil, too. We need clean soil to grow food.

Recycle.

A lot of trash can be turned into new things. Bottles, boxes, cans, and jars can be recycled.

Drive cars less.

Cars cause a lot of pollution. Riding on a bus causes less pollution. Riding a bike does not pollute at all!

What can you do to help?

Use less electricity.

Coal is burned to make electricity. Burning coal causes pollution. If we use less electricity, then less coal needs to be burned.

Use nontoxic cleaners.

Many cleaners are toxic. That means they pollute the water when they go down the drain. Nontoxic cleaners are safe to use.

Help clean up.

Be sure to put all your trash in garbage cans. Don't be a litterbug! Whenever you can, help clean up the litter you see.

Plant trees.

Trees help clean the air. The more trees there are, the cleaner the air will be!

Think and Solve

Study the infographic. Answer the questions.

1. How many ways to help stop pollution are shown in the infographic?

_____

2. How does planting a tree help with pollution?

_____

3. Riding a bike causes pollution.

True   **False**

Collect Data

How much do you help clean up the planet? For one week, keep track using tally marks. Each time you do one of the things below, make a mark.

Key				
| = 1	|| = 2	||| = 3	|||| = 4	⦀⦀ = 5

Recycle a can, bottle, box, or other item.	Turn off lights when you leave a room.	Pick up litter.	Use a nontoxic cleaner.

Make a Bar Graph

How much did you help the clean-up crew? Count the tally marks in your chart. Start at the bottom of the graph. For each tally mark, color in one section of the graph.

Recycle   **Turn off lights**   **Clean up**   **Use nontoxic cleaners**

Draw It

Which activity did you do most often? Draw a picture of yourself doing it.

Animals of Africa

This map shows some of Africa's animals and where you can see them in the wild. The population in the wild for each animal is also given.

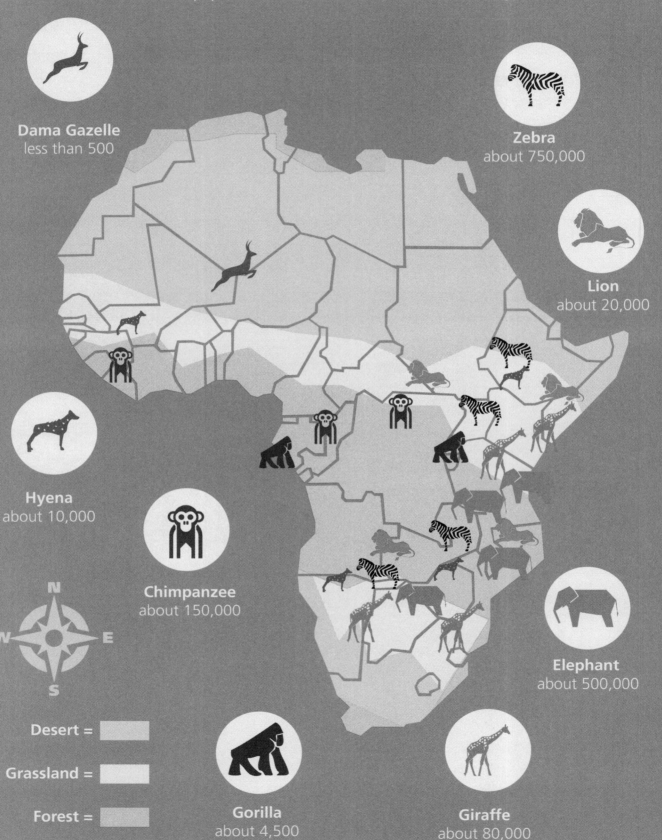

Dama Gazelle
less than 500

Zebra
about 750,000

Lion
about 20,000

Hyena
about 10,000

Chimpanzee
about 150,000

Elephant
about 500,000

Desert =

Grassland =

Forest =

Gorilla
about 4,500

Giraffe
about 80,000

Think and Solve

Study the infographic. Answer the questions.

1. There are more elephants in Africa than any other animal.

True   **False**

2. Which animal has the smallest population?

_____

3. The northern part of Africa is mostly (forest, desert).

_____

4. Write the population for each animal.

Gorilla _____   Lion _____

Hyena _____   Chimpanzee _____

Make a Chart

For each animal, draw an X in the chart to show where it lives. Some animals will need more than one X.

	Lion	Elephant	Dama Gazelle	Hyena	Chimpanzee
Desert					
Grassland					
Forest					

Pictures From the Dawn of Time

A *petroglyph* is a picture or symbol on a rock. The image can be carved, scratched, or chipped into the rock. Petroglyphs have been found all over the world.

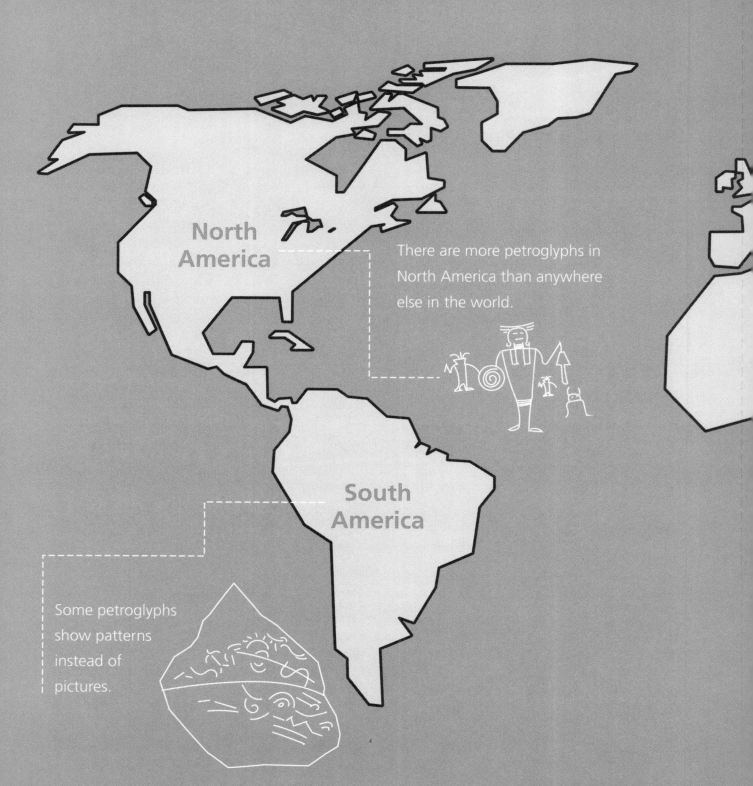

North America

There are more petroglyphs in North America than anywhere else in the world.

South America

Some petroglyphs show patterns instead of pictures.

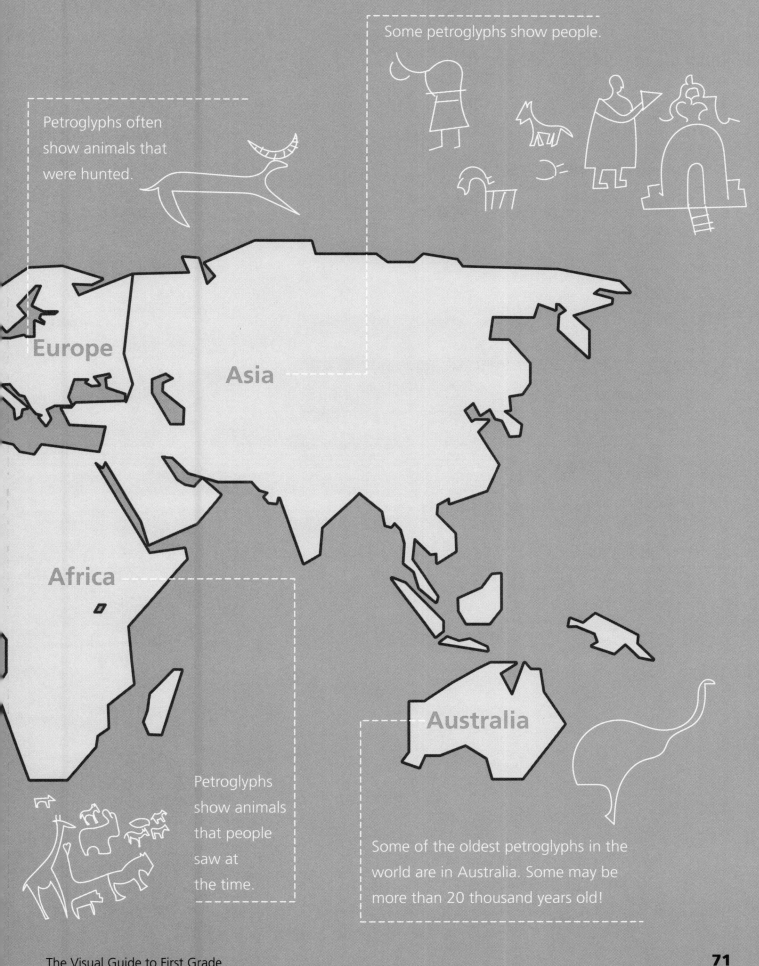

Some petroglyphs show people.

Petroglyphs often show animals that were hunted.

Europe

Asia

Africa

Petroglyphs show animals that people saw at the time.

Australia

Some of the oldest petroglyphs in the world are in Australia. Some may be more than 20 thousand years old!

Think and Solve

Study the infographic. Answer the questions.

1. Some petroglyphs show patterns instead of pictures.
   True   **False**

2. There are more petroglyphs in _____ than anywhere else.

3. The oldest petroglyphs are more than _____ years old.
   A. 2,000,000
   B. 200,000
   C. 20,000
   D. 2,000

4. Why do you think ancient people made petroglyphs?

   _____

   _____

Read About It: Petroglyphs

Study the petroglyphs and their meanings. You will use them to make a story on the next page.

Draw and Write

Use the petroglyphs from page 72 to tell a story. Draw petroglyphs in the boxes. Write a sentence under each box. Share your story with a friend.

Eclipses

An *eclipse* happens when the Sun, the Moon, and Earth all form a line. Eclipses can be lunar or solar. The type of eclipse depends on where the Moon and Earth are in their orbits.

Solar Eclipse

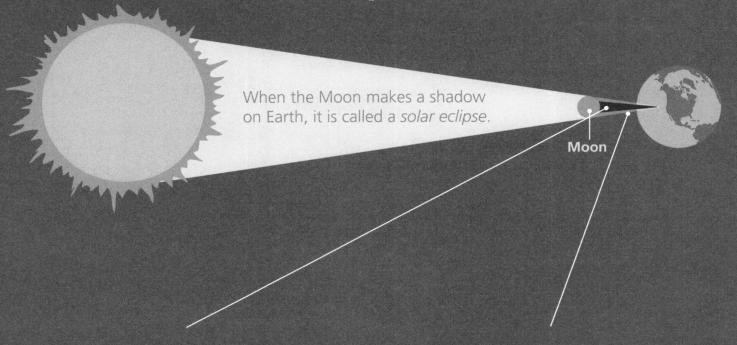

When the Moon makes a shadow on Earth, it is called a *solar eclipse*.

Moon

The darkest part of the shadow is small. It makes a total solar eclipse.

The lighter parts of the shadow are larger. They make a partial solar eclipse.

It is always dangerous to look at the Sun. Never look at the Sun during a solar eclipse.

Lunar Eclipse

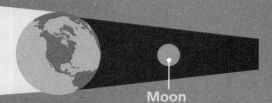

When Earth makes a shadow on the Moon, it is called a *lunar eclipse*.

Moon

When Earth's shadow covers all of the Moon, it is a total lunar eclipse. The Moon looks red.

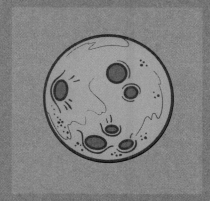

When part of Earth's shadow covers the Moon, it is a partial lunar eclipse.

It is always safe to look at the Moon. You can look at the Moon during a lunar eclipse.

Think and Solve

Study the infographic. Answer the questions.

1. The Moon looks _____ during a total lunar eclipse.

2. When the Moon makes a shadow on Earth, it is called a _____.
   A. full moon
   B. lunar eclipse
   C. solar eclipse
   D. partial lunar eclipse

3. You should never look directly at the Sun.
   True   **False**

Do the Math

The dates in the chart show when total solar eclipses and total lunar eclipses will happen. How old will you be for each one? Write your answers in the chart.

Total Eclipses	
Date	**Your Age**
July 2, 2019 (solar)	
May 26, 2021 (lunar)	
November 8, 2022 (lunar)	
April 8, 2024 (solar)	

Try It Yourself

Try this experiment to make your own solar eclipse.

What you need:

- a flashlight (to stand for the Sun)
- a baseball or other small ball (to stand for Earth)
- a ball of clay, about half the size of the baseball (to stand for the Moon)
- a ruler or measuring tape

What you do:

1. Line up the ball (Earth) and the clay (the Moon) on a table. They should be about eight inches apart.

2. Stand about two feet away from the table. Shine the flashlight (the Sun) so it is at the same level as the clay (the Moon) and the ball (Earth). Then, shine the light from behind the clay (the Moon).

3. You will see a shadow on the ball (Earth). When the Moon blocks the Sun's light, it makes a shadow on Earth. This is how a solar eclipse happens!

Write About It

Write about what happened when you tried the experiment.

_____

_____

_____

_____

Long Jumpers

How far can these animals jump
in a singe leap?

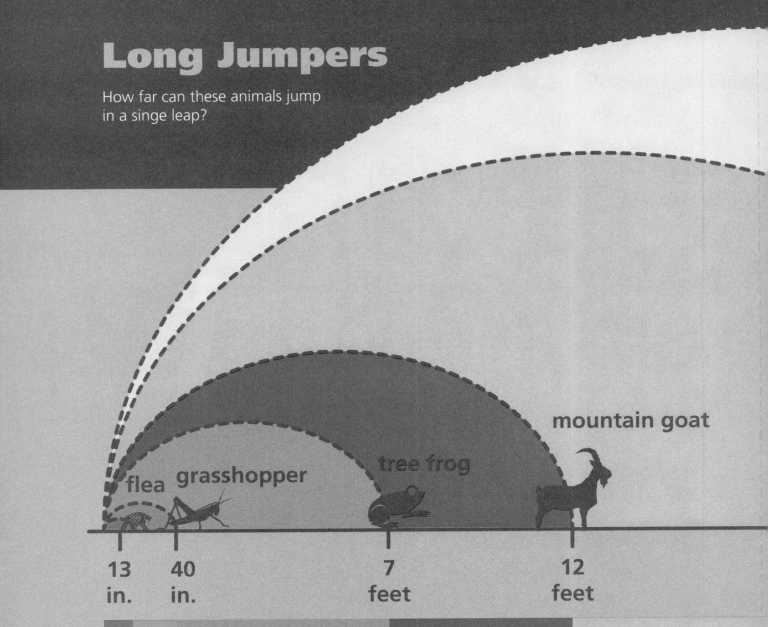

flea **grasshopper** **tree frog** **mountain goat**

13 in.   40 in.   7 feet   12 feet

Fleas can jump 200 times the length of their own bodies.

A grasshopper's muscular back legs allow it to leap 20 times its body length.

Tree frogs have webbed toes that act as parachutes to slow their fall.

Mountain goats jump from one rocky mountain ledge to the next.

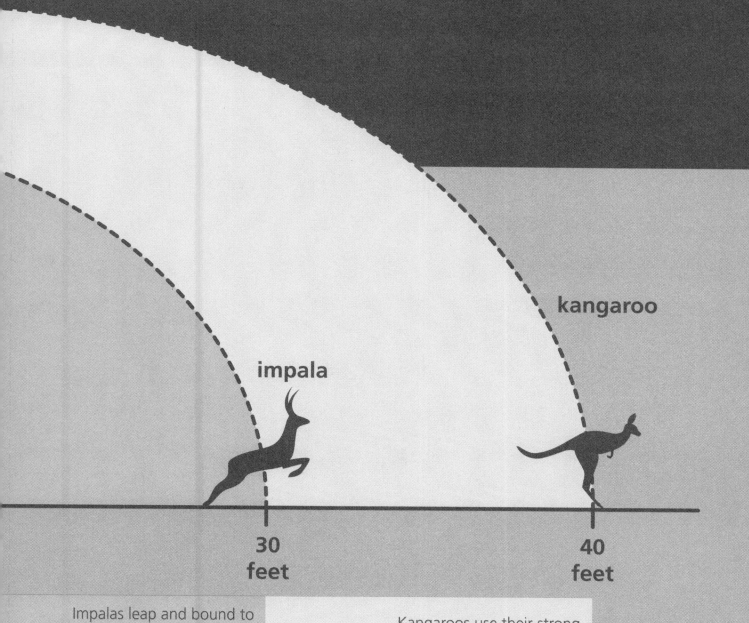

kangaroo

impala

30
feet

40
feet

Impalas leap and bound to escape predators or sometimes just for fun!

Kangaroos use their strong tails for balance while jumping.

How far can you jump?

To leap like an Olympic long jumper, get a running start before springing forward onto a soft surface. Record-breaking athletes have jumped as far as 30 feet!

30! FT.!

Think and Solve

Study the infographic. Answer the questions.

1. How many mammals are shown in the infographic?

_____

2. Which animal jumps farther than a record-breaking human athlete?

_____

3. A snow leopard can jump as far as 50 feet. Where would a snow leopard appear in the infographic?

_____

Do the Math

Solve the problems. Use the infographic to help you.

1. A grasshopper can jump more than _____ feet.
(Hint: 1 foot = 12 inches)

   A. 3

   B. 13

   C. 36

   D. 48

2. A tree frog jumps two times.
How many feet does it jump in all?

_____ feet

3. How much farther can a kangaroo jump than a mountain goat?

_____ feet

4. A mountain goat jumps three times. How many feet does it jump in all?

_____ feet

Identify It

Imagine the animals in each pair had a jumping contest. For each contest, circle the winner.

tree frog   vs.   grasshopper

mountain goat   vs.   human

human   vs.   kangaroo

grasshopper   vs.   flea

Try It Yourself

How far can you jump? To find out, follow the directions.

First, find a good place to jump. It should have soft ground, sand, or grass. Be sure there is nothing in the way. Use a stick to mark a starting line on the ground.

Get a running start. Then, jump when you reach the starting line. Look for a mark in the soft ground where you land. How many feet did you jump? Use a measuring tape to measure from the starting line to the mark. Jump two more times the same way. On each graph, use a curved line to show how far you jumped.

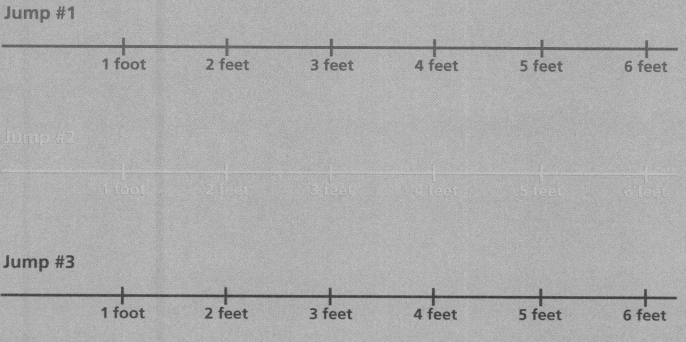

Jump #1

1 foot   2 feet   3 feet   4 feet   5 feet   6 feet

Jump #2

1 foot   2 feet   3 feet   4 feet   5 feet   6 feet

Jump #3

1 foot   2 feet   3 feet   4 feet   5 feet   6 feet

Johnny Appleseed

Have you ever heard of Johnny Appleseed?
He was both a legend and a real man. Think
of him the next time you bite into a juicy apple!

The story of Johnny Appleseed is an American legend. A *legend* is a story that has been passed down by people over many years. Legends are not all true. Some parts of them are facts. Some parts of them are made up. This makes the story more interesting. John Chapman was a real person. The legend of Johnny Appleseed is based on him. Stories about Daniel Boone, Davy Crockett, and John Henry are other famous American legends.

Johnny Appleseed was a legend. The real man was John Chapman.

Johnny loved animals. He did not eat meat.

Johnny's Apple Nurseries

IL IN OH PA

KY

Johnny was peaceful. He made friends with many American Indians.

Johnny loved nature. He liked to sleep under the stars.

Johnny died at the age of 71. People say he had never been sick before.

Johnny made money from his apples. He often gave it to the poor.

He was born in 1774.

He owned more than 1,200 acres by the age of 70.

= 100 acres

Johnny sold apple seedlings to settlers. Now, they could start orchards.

Johnny went west on foot. He planted apple seeds along the way.

He was known for dressing oddly. He wore old clothes and often had bare feet.

Think and Solve

Study the infographic. Answer the questions.

1. Name an American legend other than Johnny Appleseed.

_____

2. Johnny Appleseed planted apple trees in _____ states.
    A. three
    B. two
    C. five
    D. no

3. Johnny Appleseed traveled on foot.
    True   **False**

4. What was Johnny Appleseed's real name?

_____

Finish the Pattern

Draw the next apple in each pattern.

1.  _____

2.  _____

3.  _____

Do the Math

= 1 gallon of apple juice

Key ![apple] = 5 apples

1. How many apples are needed to make one gallon of juice?

_____ apples

2. How many apples are needed to make two gallons of juice?

_____ apples

3. How many apples are needed to make half a gallon of juice?

_____ apples

Puzzle It

Circle words about apples in the puzzle. Then, write the extra letters in order on the lines below. They will spell the answer to the riddle.

| pie | seeds | skin | core |

A	C	O	R	E
S	E	E	D	S
K	C	R	P	A
I	B	A	I	P
N	P	L	E	E

What do you get if you cross an apple with a shellfish?

_____ _____ _____ _____ _____ _____ _____ _____ _____ _____!

Chomp, Chomp

You use your teeth every day. How much do you know about your pearly whites?

■ = **molars**

Molars are wide and strong. They have lots of ridges. They work to crush and grind your food. This makes it easier to swallow.

■ = **canines**

Canines are a bit pointy and sharp. They are used for tearing food.

□ = **incisors**

Your front teeth are incisors. You have four on top and four on the bottom. They are used for cutting and chopping.

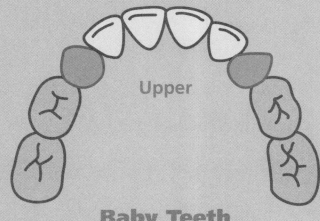

Upper

Baby Teeth

Lower

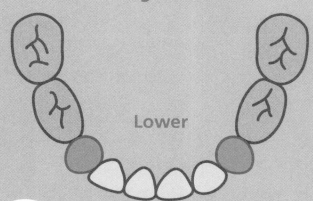

Humans have 20 baby teeth. We have 32 grown-up teeth.

Teeth help you chew, but they also help you talk. Talking without teeth would be hard!

Another name for baby teeth is milk teeth.

Teeth are covered with enamel. Enamel is hard and strong. It protects your teeth.

Tooth prints are like fingerprints. They are different for every person.

The Teeth They Need

If you are a rodent (like a squirrel, mouse, rabbit, or beaver), you have long incisors. They keep growing and must be worn down.

If you are a snake, you may have long fangs. Fangs are hollow. They are used to deliver venom when a snake bites.

If you are a cow, you only have incisors (front teeth) on the bottom! Cows chew grass side to side with their back teeth.

If you are a baleen whale, you have plates with ridges on them for teeth. (Picture the teeth of a comb.) These ridges help the whales strain water and capture tiny sea animals to eat.

If you are a shark, you might have 3,000 teeth at one time! Shark use their teeth to tear, not chew. When they lose a tooth, they just grow another one.

If you are an elephant, you have the longest teeth in the world—tusks! Tusks are very large incisors. They can be used for protection, digging, and other tasks.

Think and Solve

Study the infographic. Answer the questions.

1. A rodent's teeth keep growing. They must be worn down.

True   **False**

2. Look at the tooth diagram. What color are canines?

_____

3. How many more grown-up teeth will you have than baby teeth?

A. 32
B. 20
C. 12
D. 6

4. How are tooth prints and fingerprints alike?

_____

_____

Match It

Draw a line to match each description to the correct animal.

incisors keep growing

long, hollow fangs

front teeth only on the bottom

teeth like the teeth of a comb

Do the Math

The web shows how many teeth different types of animals have.
Use it to answer the questions below.

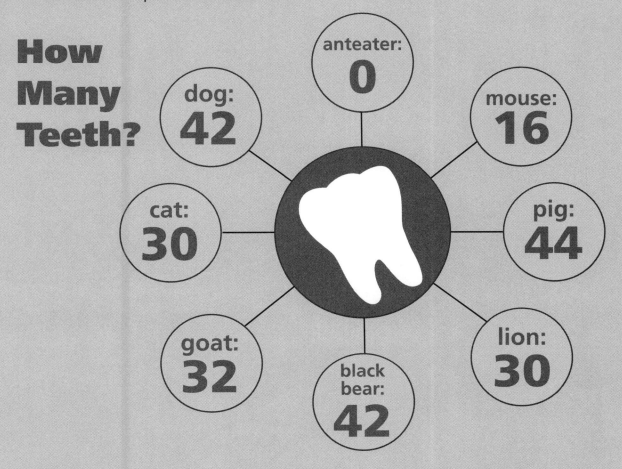

How Many Teeth?

dog: 42

anteater: 0

mouse: 16

cat: 30

pig: 44

goat: 32

black bear: 42

lion: 30

1. Which animal pairs have the same number of teeth?

_____ and _____

_____ and _____

2. A pig has _____ more teeth than a black bear.

3. Two goats together have _____ teeth.

4. A lion has _____ more teeth than an anteater.

5. Number the animals below in order, from least to most teeth.

_____ pigs _____ cats _____ dogs _____ mice

Totem Poles

Totem poles have different uses. They can mark graves. They can hold up the roof of a house. They can show who owns a piece of land.

Totem poles are carved and painted logs. They are part of American Indian culture in the Northwest part of North America.

Most totem poles are 10 to 30 feet tall.

An eagle's beak is always curved down on a totem pole.

The animals on a totem pole are symbols. They represent the family who owns the pole.

Some totem poles are more than 50 feet tall. That is higher than a 5-story building!

Totem poles do not last forever. The wet climate in the Northwest rots the wood. Most totem poles fall down after about 65 years.

$3,000 PER FOOT

Totem poles were a sign of wealth. It costs from $50 to $3,000 for each foot of height.

Piece It Together

Make your own totem pole. Think about which animals you will use. Which ones say something about you or your family?

Cut apart all the pieces. Use the blanks to draw your own animals, people, or designs. Then, choose five of the pieces for your totem pole. Include at least one piece that you drew yourself. Glue or tape the pieces you choose in a stack on page 93.

Eagle

Wolf

Raven

Bear

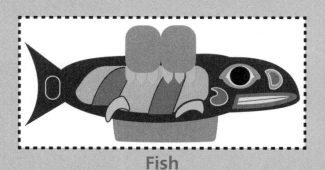
Fish

Frog

My Own Totem Pole

Write About It

What does your totem pole mean to you? Write about each part of your totem pole.

_____

_____

_____

_____

_____

_____

_____

_____

The Power of Wind

Wind is a powerful force on Earth. During a storm, wind can cause damage.
When it powers a wind turbine, wind helps people.

The Beaufort Wind Scale measures wind power.

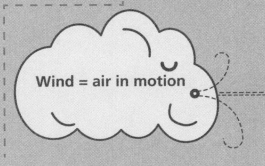

Wind = air in motion

2

4–7 mph
Leaves rustle

5

19–24 mph
Small trees sway

How does wind form?

Hot air rises, and cool air falls. When
warm air rises, cool air moves in to take
its place. This movement of air
creates wind.

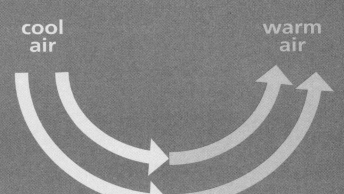

cool air

warm air

How does a wind turbine work?

1. Wind blows against the blades.
2. Wind makes the blades turn.
3. The turning blades make gears spin very fast.
4. The gears spin the generator. The generator spins and makes electricity.
5. The electricity moves through a cable.
6. The electricity travels to people's homes.

A *hurricane* is a huge storm that forms over the ocean. Hurricanes have very strong winds. When a hurricane reaches land, it can cause terrible destruction.

Hurricane	Year	Top Wind Speed
Patricia	2015	200 mph
Allen	1980	190 mph
Wilma	2005	183 mph
Rita	2005	177 mph

9

47–54 mph
Light damage

11

64–72 mph
Lots of damage

12

73+ mph
Extreme destruction

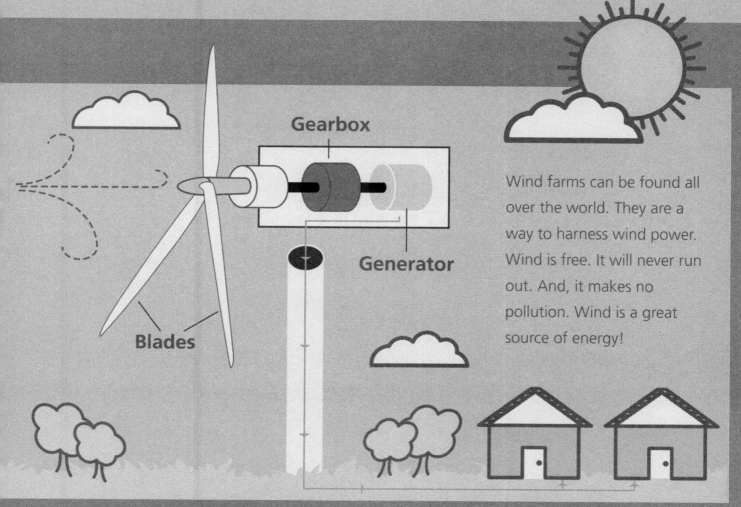

Gearbox

Generator

Blades

Wind farms can be found all over the world. They are a way to harness wind power. Wind is free. It will never run out. And, it makes no pollution. Wind is a great source of energy!

Think and Solve

Study the infographic. Answer the questions.

1. If the wind is blowing at 20 mph, what would it measure on the Beaufort Wind Scale?

_____

2. What happens when hot air rises?

_____

3. In what order are the hurricanes listed in the infographic?

  A. alphabetical

  B. the years when they happened

  C. how strong the winds were

  D. how long the hurricane lasted

4. Wind is moving air.

  True   **False**

Explore Your World

Can you see wind? No, but you can see what it does. Go outside and look for the wind. Circle the signs of wind you see.

leaves rustling   **clouds moving**

a flag waving   **branches swaying**

your hair moving   **wind chimes dinging**

paper flying   **water rippling**

Make a Pinwheel

Follow the directions to make a pinwheel.

What you need:
- an adult's help
- scissors
- a pin or tack
- a pencil with an eraser

What you do:
1. Cut out the square on this page.
2. Use a pin or tack to poke a hole in the center of each dot.
3. Cut along each line. Be sure to stop cutting where the line ends.
4. Bend each corner toward the middle. The holes in the corners will line up with the hole in the middle.

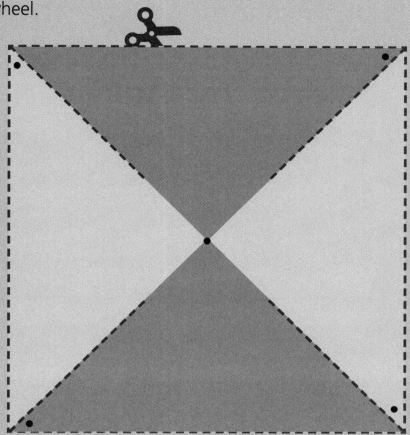

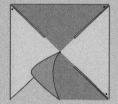

5. Push the pin or tack through the holes at the center.

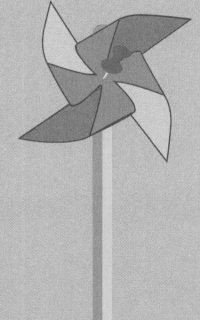

6. Push the pin or tack into the pencil's eraser. Do not push the pin or tack in tight. The pinwheel needs room to spin.

7. Blow on the pinwheel. If it does not spin, the pin or tack may be pushed in too tight.

Collect Data

Which way does the wind blow? Use your pinwheel to find out.

Ask an adult to help you draw a compass on a piece of cardboard. Use the compass pictures on this page as a guide. Go outside and find an open area. Place the compass on the ground. Have an adult help you turn it so the *N* is pointing north. Stand on the compass.

Hold your pinwheel in front of you. It will spin fastest when it is pointed at the wind. Turn until you are facing the wind and the pinwheel is spinning as fast as it can. Then, turn around and face the opposite way. Look down at the compass. You will see the direction in which the wind is blowing.

Each day for six days, check the wind's direction. Choose the same time to check the wind each day. Late afternoon is often the windiest part of the day. Show the wind's direction each day by drawing an arrow on a compass below.

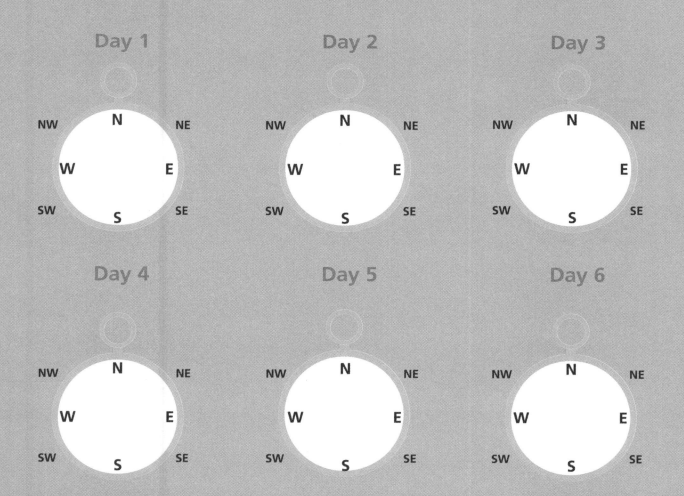

Scorpions

Scorpions are tough, fierce creatures. They live all around the world.

Where Scorpions Live

North America
Europe
Asia
Africa
South America
Australia
Antarctica

= scorpions

Colors of Scorpions

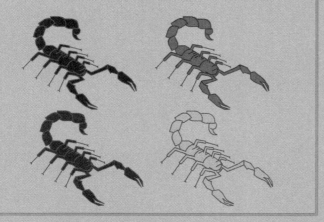

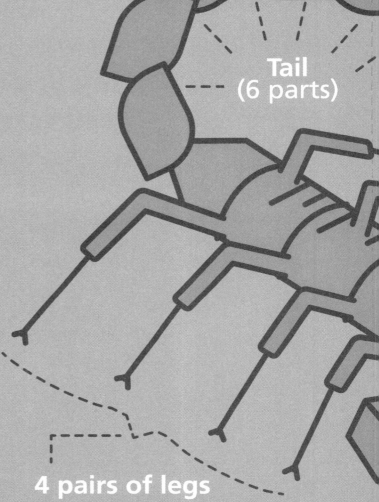

Tail (6 parts)

4 pairs of legs

spider   tick

The biggest scorpion is the emperor scorpion. It lives in rain forests in Africa. It is about 8 inches long. That's about as long as a new pencil!

Scorpions are arachnids. Arachnids have 8 legs. Spiders and ticks are also arachnids. Arachnids are not insects. Insects have only 6 legs.

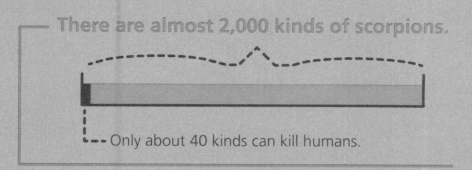

There are almost 2,000 kinds of scorpions.

Only about 40 kinds can kill humans.

Stinger

A scorpion's tail has a stinger. The stinger has venom in it. A scorpion uses its stinger to kill prey. It uses its stinger when it is in danger, too.

Scorpions are tough! Scientists froze some overnight. The next day, they put the scorpions in the sun. They thawed out and were okay!

Mouth

A scorpion's venom turns its prey's insides into liquid. Then, the scorpion can suck them up.

Scorpions are *nocturnal*. That means they hide and sleep during the day. They are active at night.

2 Claws

Scorpions use their claws to grab prey.

Think and Solve

Study the infographic. Answer the questions.

1. A scorpion's tail has _____ parts.

2. Most scorpions are deadly to humans.

True   **False**

3. Scorpions live on all continents except _____.

    A. North America

    B. Antarctica

    C. Australia

    D. Europe

4. What does it mean to say that scorpions are *nocturnal*?

_____

Do the Math

Solve the problems. Use the infographic to help you.

1. How many legs do two scorpions have?

_____

2. The largest type of scorpion is eight inches long. How much shorter is this than one foot? (Hint: 1 foot = 12 inches)

_____ inches

3. A scorpion, a spider, and a ladybug have _____ legs altogether.

    A. 16

    B. 20

    C. 22

    D. 28

Classify It

Write the name of each creature under the correct heading.

scorpion

beetle

ant

spider

tick

bumblebee

mite

grasshopper

Arachnids

Insects

_____

_____

_____

_____

_____

_____

_____

_____

Where's the Answer?

How far is it to the moon?

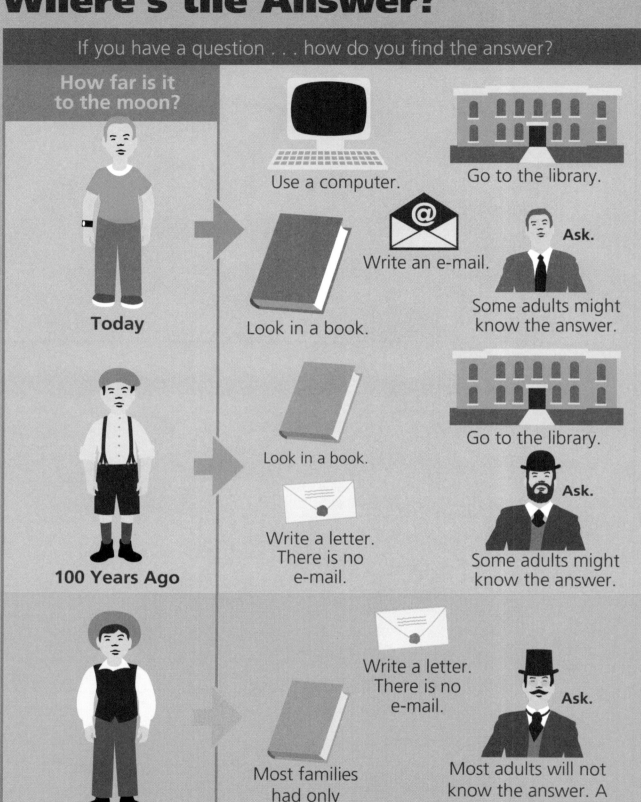

Today

Use a computer.

Go to the library.

Look in a book.

Write an e-mail.

Ask.

Some adults might know the answer.

100 Years Ago

Look in a book.

Write a letter. There is no e-mail.

Go to the library.

Ask.

Some adults might know the answer.

200 Years Ago

Most families had only one book.

Write a letter. There is no e-mail.

Ask.

Most adults will not know the answer. A scientist might.

By the way, the moon is about 240,000 miles from Earth!

Think and Solve
Study the infographic. Answer the questions.

1. Libraries did not exist 100 years ago.

   True   **False**

2. You want to know today how much an elephant weighs. Where could you find the answer?

   _____

3. Imagine you are living 200 years ago. You want to know how to bake bread. How do you find the answer?

   _____

   _____

Match It
Draw a line to match each question to the best place to find the answer.

How many tablespoons are in one cup?

What countries border France?

What does the word *stubborn* mean?

What year did my grandparents come to America?

Where Did You Get That Shirt?

A T-shirt is made from cotton. Cotton is a plant that grows in the ground. How does a plant become a shirt?

HARVEST
Fluffy cotton bolls are picked by hand or by machine.

9,000,000
In one year, a single cotton farm can produce enough cotton to make more than 9 million T-shirts!

GIN
The cotton gin separates the cotton from the seed. The clean cotton is then pressed into bales.

SPIN
Next, machines turn the cotton into yarn. (It's called yarn, but it's more like thread.) It is wound on large spools.

KNIT
Now, the yarn is knit into cloth on huge looms.

There are about 6 miles of yarn in a single T-shirt!

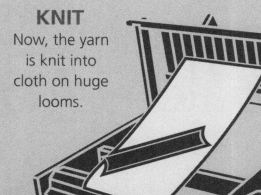

FINISH
The cloth is washed and shrunk. Before this step, it is rough and grayish.

Eli Whitney
invented the cotton gin in 1793. Before the cotton gin, cotton had to be separated by hand!

CUT
The shirts are cut. Usually, they are stacked first. Machines do the cutting.

DYE
The last step is to dye the shirts. Sometimes, this is done in the same step as the finishing. Now, the shirts are ready to be sold!

SEW
The sleeves and collars are sewn to the body of the shirt. Sewers work at machines, often in a factory.

Think and Solve

Study the infographic. Answer the questions.

1. A cotton gin separates the _____ from the _____.

2. What is a loom used for?

    A. to clean cotton

    B. to make cloth

    C. to dye shirts

    D. to cut cloth

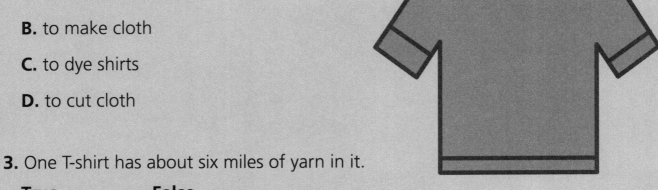

3. One T-shirt has about six miles of yarn in it.

    True   **False**

4. The steps needed to make a shirt are shown below.

    Number them in order from 1 to 8.

_____ Sew		_____ Harvest
_____ Spin		_____ Finish
_____ Knit		_____ Cut
_____ Gin		_____ Dye

5. What happens when the cloth is washed?

    A. The cloth turns gray and rough.

    B. The cotton separates from the seed.

    C. It becomes softer.

    D. The cloth is folded and cut.

Make a Process Chart

What do you know how to make or do? Read the list of ideas.
Make a check mark beside the one that you will explain how to do.

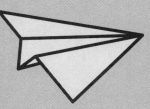

☐ Make a sandwich.

☐ Plant a flower.

☐ Play a prank.

☐ Make breakfast.

☐ Make a paper airplane.

☐ Make a bed.

☐ Fold a shirt.

☐ Make a fairy house.

Now, tell how to make or do the thing you checked. Write it on the line. Then, draw and write one step in each box. The arrows show the order of the steps. You may not use all the boxes. If you need more boxes, draw them on another sheet of paper.

How to _____

```
┌──────────┐      ┌──────────┐      ┌──────────┐
│          │  →   │          │  →   │          │
│          │      │          │      │          │
└──────────┘      └──────────┘      └──────────┘
                                         ↓
┌──────────┐      ┌──────────┐      ┌──────────┐
│          │  ←   │          │  ←   │          │
│          │      │          │      │          │
└──────────┘      └──────────┘      └──────────┘
```

Night Critters

Some animals sleep for most of the day. At night, they wake up. They are active while you sleep. They are called *nocturnal animals*. Who are these night creatures?

Fireflies are insects that make their own light. The lights can be yellow, orange, or green.

Bats are the only mammals that can fly. One bat can eat 1,000 insects an hour!

Toads come out at night to hunt for insects. Toads often sit under lights. They catch and eat bugs that fly there.

Only male crickets chirp. They make the noise by rubbing their wings together.

Like raccoons, foxes are omnivores. When it is cold, a fox will use its tail like a blanket.

Opossums are scavengers. They eat animals that are already dead. They dig through garbage for food.

Luna moths fly only at night. They do not have mouths because they do not eat. They live for only one week.

Barred owls are carnivores. They hunt other animals for food.

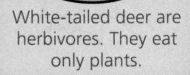

Like owls, bobcats are carnivores. They are about twice as big as a housecat. Bobcats are very shy. People do not see them very often in the wild.

Raccoons are omnivores. They eat both plants and animals.

White-tailed deer are herbivores. They eat only plants.

Think and Solve

Study the infographic. Answer the questions.

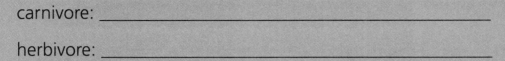

1. Write one example for each type of animal.

carnivore: _____

herbivore: _____

omnivore: _____

2. How many insects are shown in the infographic?

_____

3. Bats are the only nocturnal animals that fly.
True   **False**

4. Why do toads often sit under lights?

_____

Match It

Look at the footprints. Match each set of footprints to the animal that made them.

deer

toad

owl

raccoon

bobcat

Explore Your World

Who visits your neighborhood at night? Follow the directions to find out.

What you need:
- an old white sheet
- food scraps

What you do:

1. Find a flat place in your yard or neighborhood. A place with more dirt and less grass will work best.

2. Lay out the sheet.

3. Carefully place food in the middle. Bread crusts are good. Fruit will work, too. Peanut butter is another great idea. Try not to walk all over the sheet. You don't need to collect your own footprints!

4. Make the area around the sheet muddy. Use a watering can or hose.

5. Leave everything there overnight.

6. The next day, see who came to eat. The night critters' footprints will be on the sheet.

Whose footprints did you see? Draw the footprints in the boxes below.

How many animals visited during the night? _____

What animals made the footprints? If you are not sure, check a field guide or an approved website.

_____   _____   _____

Going Bananas

Bananas may be the perfect food. They are tasty. They are packed with vitamins. They even come in their own sealed package!

Bananas are cut into clusters. There are 4–10 bananas in each. Next, they are washed and packed.

The inside of a banana peel can be used to polish shoes!

Most of the bananas we eat are a type called *Cavendish*.

It looks like bananas grow on trees. They are really huge herb plants!

Bananas start to get sweeter after they are cut.

There are about 400 types of bananas!

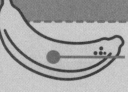

One banana is known as a *finger*.

A bunch is called a *hand*.

In the US, each person eats about 27 pounds of bananas a year!

While they grow, bananas are covered with a bag. This keeps them safe from sun and bugs.

Bananas grow in warm, tropical places. They grow well where it rains a lot.

Bananas grow in at least 107 countries.

To help bananas ripen, place them in a paper bag.

In the state of Washington, you can visit a banana museum!

Bananas travel on a cooled ship. This keeps them from getting ripe too fast.

Banana leaves can be useful. In some places, they are used as plates. They can also be used as wrappers for food.

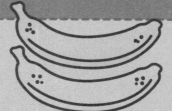

Plantains are a type of banana. They are often eaten in tropical places. They can be fried, grilled, or baked.

Do the Math

Solve the problems. Use the infographic to help you.

1. There are three bananas in each bunch. How many are there in four bunches?

_____ bananas

2. Three monkeys climbed a tree. Six more monkeys joined them.

How many monkeys were in the tree? _____ monkeys

3. A monkey grabbed 12 bunches of bananas. It dropped three bunches.

How many bunches were left? _____ bunches

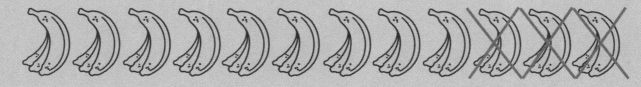

4. About how many pounds of bananas do two Americans eat in one year?

_____

Describe It

Adjectives are describing words. Choose adjectives that describe bananas.
Write them on the bananas.

salty	sweet	yellow	blue
pink	icy	soft	crunchy
fruity	spicy	long	tropical
striped	prickly	ripe	curved

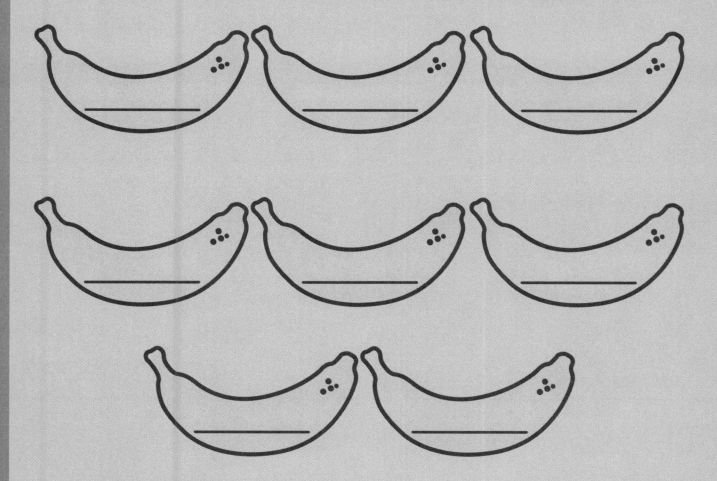

Write one more adjective that describes bananas.

_____

Burning Wild

Wildfires are out-of-control fires. They are dangerous
for people and animals.

Wildfires can start with . . .

- campfires
- burning garbage
- cigarettes
- arson (people setting fires on purpose)
- lightning
- fireworks
- lava

About 9 out of 10 wildfires
are caused by humans!

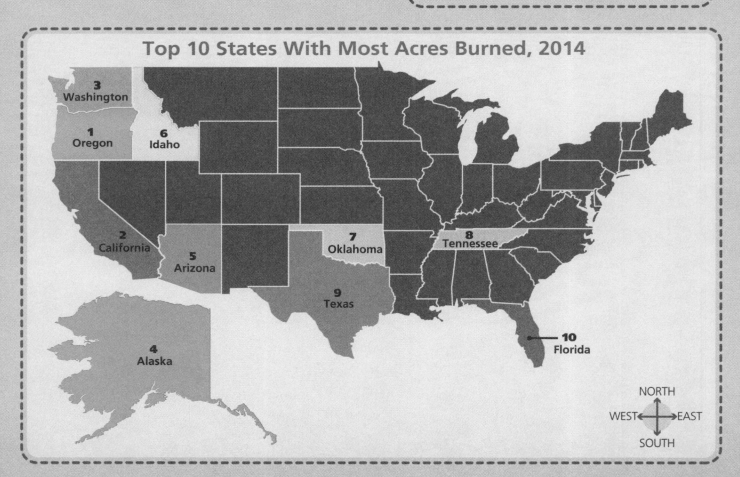

Top 10 States With Most Acres Burned, 2014

3 Washington
1 Oregon
6 Idaho
2 California
5 Arizona
7 Oklahoma
8 Tennessee
9 Texas
4 Alaska
10 Florida

NORTH
WEST — EAST
SOUTH

How to Fight a Wildfire

Firebreaks Firefighters clear a ring around the fire. When the fire gets to the ring, it has no fuel to keep burning.

Controlled Burn Firefighters look for something that might help slow the fire, like a stream or a road. Then, they burn everything between it and the fire.

Aircraft Special planes fly over. They drop water and chemicals on the fire.

Firefighters People who fight wildfires have special training. Their work is dangerous. They have special gear. They work long hours.

Types of Wildfires

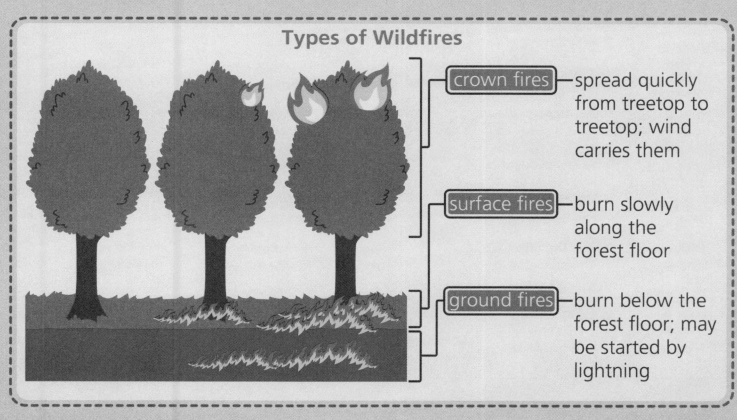

crown fires — spread quickly from treetop to treetop; wind carries them

surface fires — burn slowly along the forest floor

ground fires — burn below the forest floor; may be started by lightning

Think and Solve

Study the infographic. Answer the questions.

1. Most wildfires are not caused by humans.
True   **False**

2. Which is not a way to fight wildfires?
    A. aircraft
    B. arson
    C. firebreaks
    D. controlled burns

3. Which type of wildfire burns along treetops?

_____

4. On the map, which state has more acres burned than any other?
    A. Washington
    B. Oregon
    C. Florida
    D. Texas

Write About It

Think of a solution for each problem. Write your ideas in the chart.

Problem	Solution
People throw out lit cigarettes near woods.	
People do not put campfires out all the way.	
People burn garbage. The fires can get out of control.	

Identify It

Look at the picture. Circle five things that could start a wildfire.

The Tallest Animal on Earth

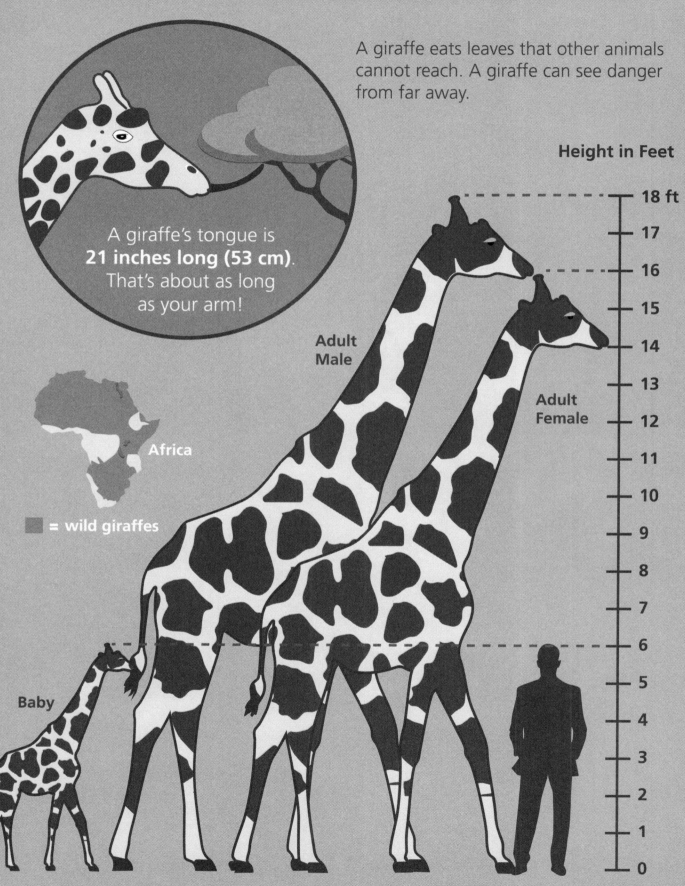

A giraffe eats leaves that other animals cannot reach. A giraffe can see danger from far away.

A giraffe's tongue is **21 inches long (53 cm)**. That's about as long as your arm!

Africa

= wild giraffes

Adult Male

Adult Female

Baby

Height in Feet

18 ft
17
16
15
14
13
12
11
10
9
8
7
6
5
4
3
2
1
0

Think and Solve

Study the infographic. Answer the questions.

1. How does a giraffe's height help it?

_____

2. An adult female giraffe is _____ feet taller than a human man.

3. Wild giraffes are found in every part of Africa.
   True   **False**

Explore Your World

What is longer than a giraffe's tongue? What is shorter than a giraffe's tongue?
Use a string to find out.

Use a ruler or a tape measure to measure 21 inches on a string. Ask an adult to help you cut the string so it is 21 inches long. Then, use your string to measure things inside and outside. Find four things that are longer than a giraffe's tongue. Find four things that are shorter than a giraffe's tongue. Write the name of each thing in the chart under the correct heading.

Shorter than a giraffe's tongue	Longer than a giraffe's tongue

To the Rescue!

Firefighters are brave men and women. For hundreds of years, they have worked hard to fight fires and save lives.

EARLY FIREFIGHTERS

Early firefighters were part of a bucket brigade. They would fill up buckets with water and pass them down the line.

Early firefighters...

...wore heavy wool clothing.

...wore helmets made of leather.

...used heavy hoses made from leather.

The horse-drawn steam pumper helped firefighters do their work. But, there was not much room for them to ride. They often had to walk or run to the fire!

The boiler held water. The water was heated and turned into steam. The steam pressure was used to turn the pump.

The pump pulled water through a hose that was attached to a hydrant. The hose was used to spray the fire.

124

TODAY'S FIREFIGHTERS

Firefighters today use powerful hoses to spray water and chemicals at fires. They also wear special clothing to protect them.

Today's firefighters...

...wear light clothing made of special plastic fabric to protect them from heat.

...wear helmets made from strong plastic.

...use light plastic hoses.

Hoses are hooked up to hydrants.

The ladder reaches up about 100 feet!

Equipment and tools are stored in the storage compartments.

The flashing lights and siren say, "Watch out! Coming through!"

The pump panel lets firefighters control the water.

The fire trucks of today have everything firefighters need to beat the flames!

Think and Solve

Study the infographic. Answer the questions.

1. What is a bucket brigade?

_____

2. Early firefighters often had to walk to fires.

True   **False**

3. What do modern fire trucks have that early steam pumpers did not?
  A. a pump
  B. wheels
  C. a driver
  D. a siren

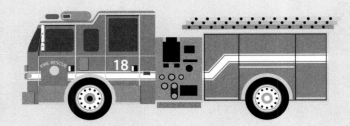

Classify It

Read the list of equipment. Write *E* if it was used by early firefighters.
Write *T* if it is used by firefighters today.

1. _____ plastic helmet

2. _____ horses

3. _____ siren

4. _____ wool clothing

5. _____ leather hoses

6. _____ bucket brigade

7. _____ light, protective clothes

8. _____ plastic hoses

Piece It Together

Cut out the firefighting equipment. Glue or tape it on page 129 to help the modern firefighter get ready to fight fires.

protective coat

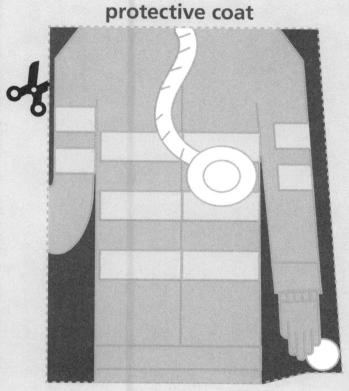

boots

axe
(used to break down doors, walls, and roofs)

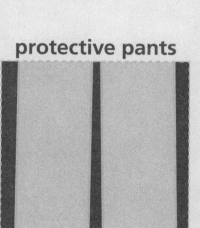

mask
(helps the firefighter breathe in smoky air)

air tank
(attached to mask)

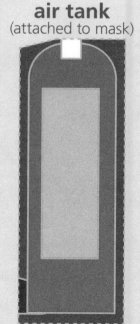

strong plastic helmet

protective pants

Ready to Fight Fires!

Inside the White House

The White House is the home of the President of the United States. The president lives and works there. When a new president is elected, the old president moves out and the new one moves in.

Every president except George Washington has lived in the White House.

President Wilson kept sheep on the White House lawn during World War I. He wanted to show his support for the troops. The sheep cut the grass for free. The sale of their wool earned money for the Red Cross.

The White House's official address

1600 Pennsylvania Avenue

The China Room displays the special dishes used by different presidents throughout history.

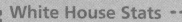

The Map Room is used for special meetings with the president. It has a collection of maps from around the world.

The Oval Office is the president's office. It really is an oval! The president often addresses the public from here.

The Rose Garden is outside the Oval Office. The garden is filled with flowers. It is often used for important events, such as when the president talks to the American people.

Think and Solve

Study the infographic. Answer the questions.

1. Are there more fireplaces or bathrooms in the White House?

_____

2. Which president did not live at the White House?

_____

3. What is the name of the street where the president lives?

_____

4. The president lives at the White House, but works in another building.

True   **False**

Match It

Draw a line from each room to the sentence that tells about it.

The Rose Garden   It holds maps from around the world.

The China Room   It is the president's office.

The Oval Office   It is where dishes are displayed.

The Map Room   It is filled with flowers.

Imagine It

Imagine you are the new US president! You decide to add three new rooms to the White House. What will they be used for? What will they look like? Draw the rooms and the things inside them. Then, write to tell about each new room.

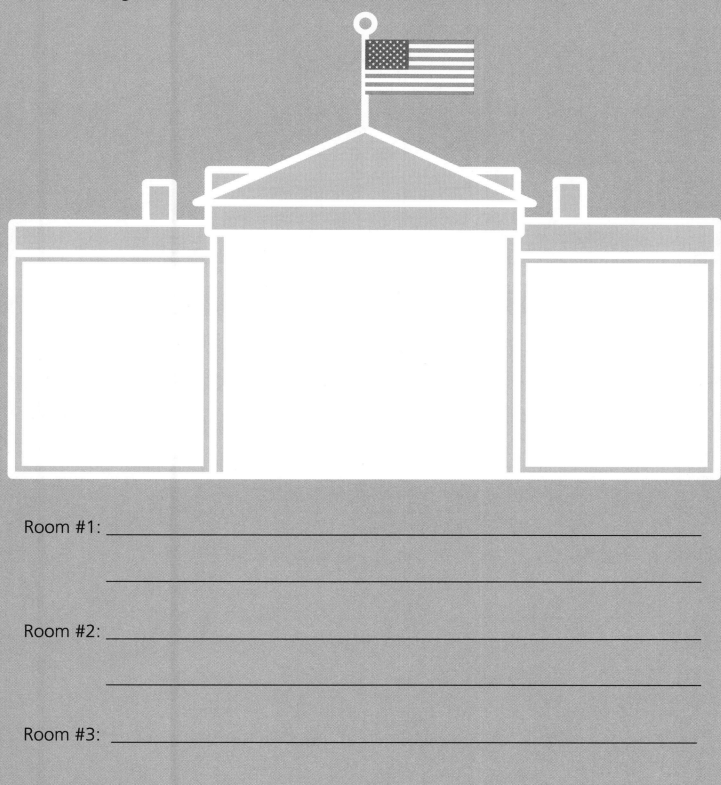

Room #1: _____

_____

Room #2: _____

_____

Room #3: _____

_____

Let's Go Spelunking!

Have you ever explored a cave deep underground?
Spelunking is a fun hobby for people who like adventure!

1. Mammoth Cave–400 miles

2. Jewel Cave–177 miles

3. Wind Cave–140 miles

4. Lechuguilla Cave–138 miles

5. Fisher Ridge Cave System–110 miles

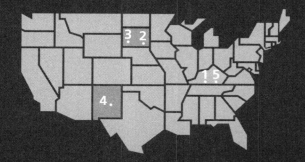

Spelunking is the exploration of caves. A person who explores caves is called a *spelunker*.

What Is Inside a Cave?

Stalactites: crystals that grow from the ceiling down; they hold *tight* to the ceiling!

Bats: often found sleeping in caves during the day

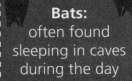

Frostwork: a type of cave crystal

Stalagmites: crystals that grow from the floor up; someday, they *might* reach the ceiling!

Cave Entrance: a covered area that animals use as shelter

Crustaceans: animals such as crabs, shrimp, and crayfish that live in some cave streams

Blind Cave Fish: fish that are blind or have no eyes at all

Think and Solve

Study the infographic. Answer the questions.

1. Where is Mammoth Cave?

   A. Kentucky

   B. South Dakota

   C. New Mexico

   D. Texas

2. Stalagmites grow up from the floor of a cave.

   True   **False**

3. How much longer is Jewel Cave than Wind Cave?

   _____ miles

4. Two caves are almost the same length. Which caves are they?

   _____ Cave and _____ Cave

Puzzle It

Find words about caves in the puzzle. Circle them.

cave	bats	stream	crystal	crab	spelunk

```
B   D   S   C   R   A   B
V   N   P   A   J   P   C
G   L   E   H   O   R   R
U   O   L   I   C   E   Y
F   Q   U   B   A   T   S
P   N   N   M   V   S   T
F   S   K   X   E   Z   A
S   T   R   E   A   M   L
```

Piece It Together

Cut out the stalactites. Glue or tape them inside the cave on page 139. Don't forget, stalactites hold **tight** to the ceiling of a cave! Arrange them in order by length, from shortest to longest.

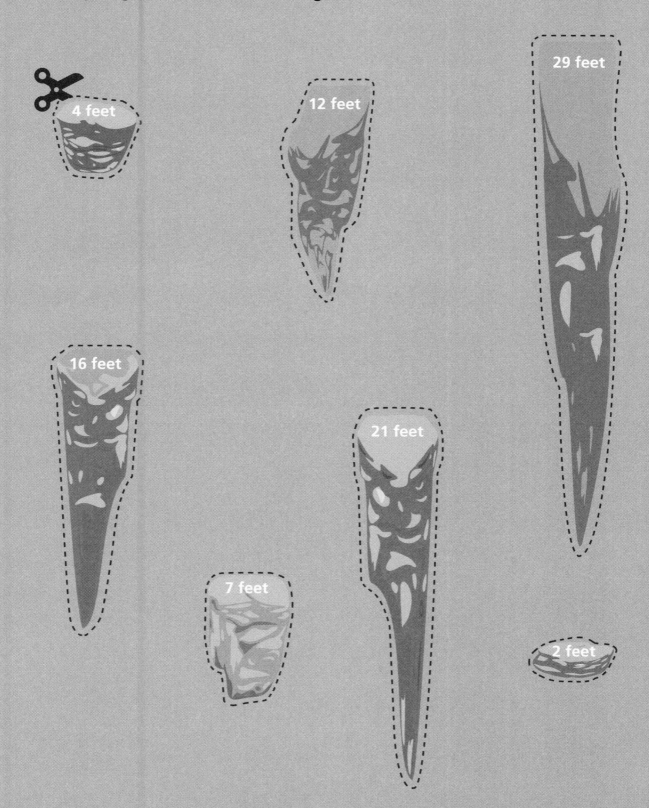

4 feet

12 feet

29 feet

16 feet

21 feet

7 feet

2 feet

Stalactites

Super Soy!

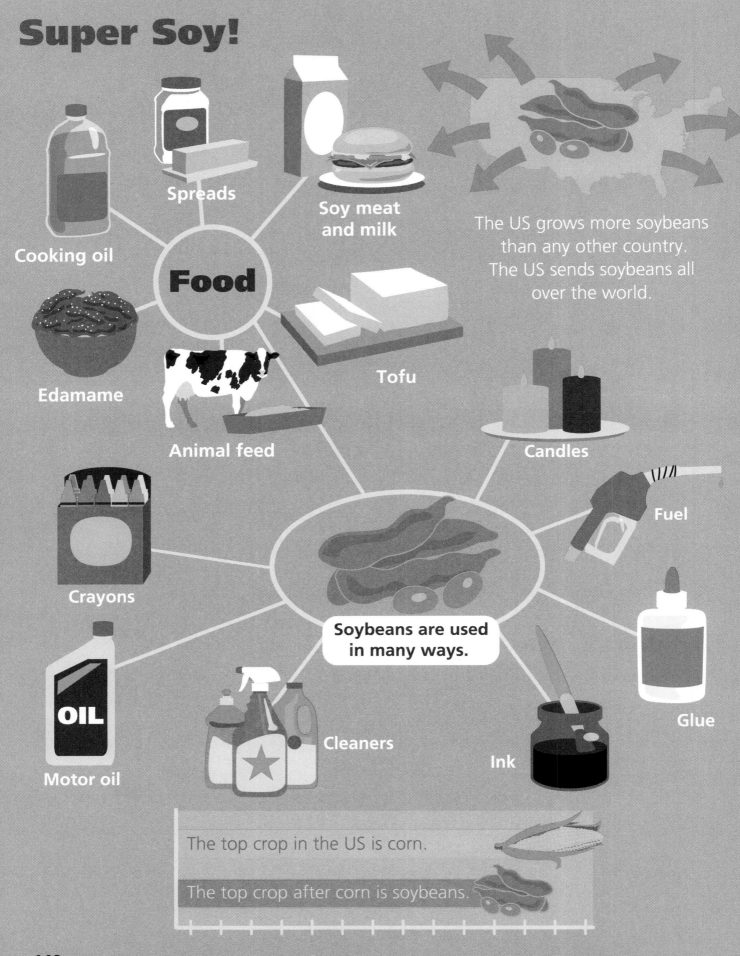

Cooking oil

Spreads

Soy meat and milk

Food

Edamame

Animal feed

Tofu

The US grows more soybeans than any other country. The US sends soybeans all over the world.

Candles

Crayons

Soybeans are used in many ways.

Fuel

Glue

Motor oil

Cleaners

Ink

The top crop in the US is corn.

The top crop after corn is soybeans.

Think and Solve

Study the infographic. Answer the questions.

1. The US grows more soybeans than any other country except China.

   True   **False**

2. List three ways soybeans are used as food.

   _____   _____   _____

3. List three ways soybeans are used other than as food.

   _____   _____   _____

4. What is the top crop grown in the US?

   _____

Explore Your World

Take a look at food products in your kitchen. Which foods have soy in them?
Read the list of ingredients on each food package closely. Look for the word *soy*.
Try to find at least five foods that have soy as an ingredient. List them below.

_____   _____   _____

_____   _____

Make Idea Webs

You know how soy is used in the US. Do you know how other crops are used? Learn more about each crop shown in an idea web on these pages. Ask an adult to help you use a book at the library or an approved website.

To complete each web, write five different ways that the crop is used. Write at least one way in which the crop is used for something other than food.

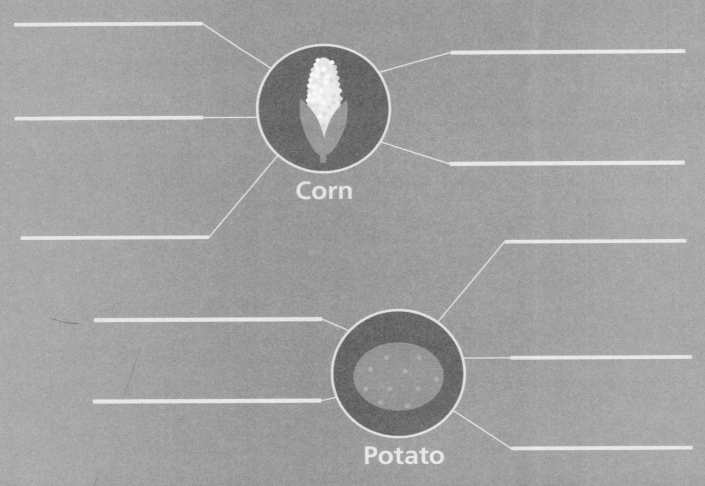

Corn

Potato

Tomato

Wheat

Look to the Stars!

A star is a giant ball of burning gases. It gives off heat and light.
Stars burn in space for a very long time. After millions and millions of years,
a star will run out of fuel. Then, the star dies.

Stars can be different temperatures.

Hottest

Blue

Blue-white

White

Yellow

Orange

Red

Coolest

Our Sun is a **yellow dwarf** star. There are many other stars like it. It is the closest star to Earth.

Dwarf stars may sound like they are little, but they are still huge. Dwarf stars got their name because they are the smallest type of stars.

Red dwarf stars are the most common stars. They burn fuel slowly. They can last for trillions of years.

A **white dwarf** star is much smaller than our Sun. White dwarfs are dying stars. As stars run out of energy, they shrink and become hotter.

Supergiants are the biggest stars. They burn a lot of fuel. They last the shortest amount of time. They can be any color.

Polaris, or the North Star, is a white supergiant. It is very big, hot, and bright.

Stars can be different sizes. Bigger stars burn out faster. Smaller stars burn out slower.

Giants are the second largest kind of star. They are 10 times brighter than our Sun. They are 100 times bigger than our Sun. They can be any color.

The second brightest star in the night sky is *Canopus*. *Canopus* is a white giant star. It can be seen from the southern parts of Earth.

Arcturus is an orange giant star. It is the brightest star in the night sky as seen from the northern parts of Earth.

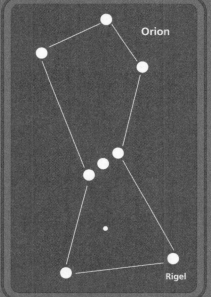

Orion

Rigel

Rigel is a blue supergiant. It is part of the Orion constellation.

Think and Solve

Study the infographic. Answer the questions.

1. Which type of star is closest to Earth?

    A. an orange giant

    B. a red supergiant

    C. a yellow dwarf

    D. a white supergiant

2. A white dwarf star is _____.

    A. a very hot, small star

    B. a cool, very large star

    C. a very hot, very large star

    D. a very cool, small star

3. The brightest star in Earth's southern skies is *Polaris*.

    True   **False**

4. Supergiants last the longest time because they have the most fuel.

    True   **False**

Sequence It

Number the stars from 1 to 6. Use 1 for the hottest star and
6 for the coolest star.

_____ _____ _____ _____ _____ _____

Explore Your World

Plan an evening of stargazing with family and friends. Make sure it is a clear night. If you can, find a place without too many lights. Then, look up into the darkness. What do you see in the night sky? In the boxes below, draw what you were able to see.

Moon

Venus
(It looks like the brightest star in the sky, but it is a planet. It is often near the Moon.)

The Constellation of Orion
(Look back to the infographic to see its shape. If you do not see Orion, draw a group of stars you do see.)

Shooting Star

Airplane

What else did you see?

Helen Keller: Growing Up

As a baby, Helen Keller lost the ability to see and hear. She grew up to be a famous writer and worked to help other people who were blind.

Helen Keller

Did you know Helen Keller...

loved dogs?

traveled the world?

could hear music by feeling the vibrations of the instrument?

was the first deaf and blind person to get a college degree?

wrote letters to eight US presidents?

VOTES FOR WOMEN

worked to get voting rights for women?

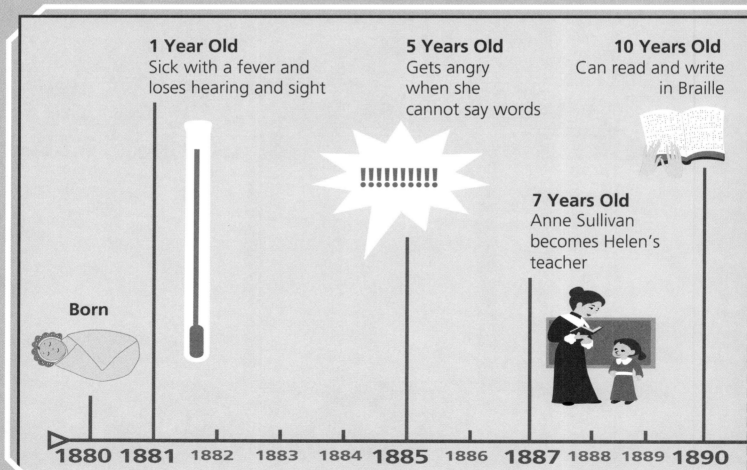

1 Year Old
Sick with a fever and loses hearing and sight

5 Years Old
Gets angry when she cannot say words

10 Years Old
Can read and write in Braille

7 Years Old
Anne Sullivan becomes Helen's teacher

Born

!!!!!!!!!!

1880 1881 1882 1883 1884 1885 1886 1887 1888 1889 1890

The Braille Alphabet

Braille is a system of dots that are raised up on paper so you can touch and feel them. It allows blind people to read words with their fingers. It was invented by a French boy, Louis Braille.

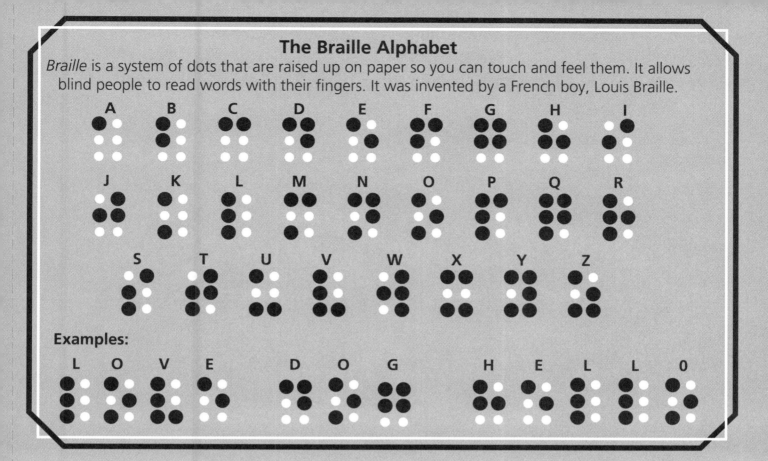

Examples:

L O V E   D O G   H E L L O

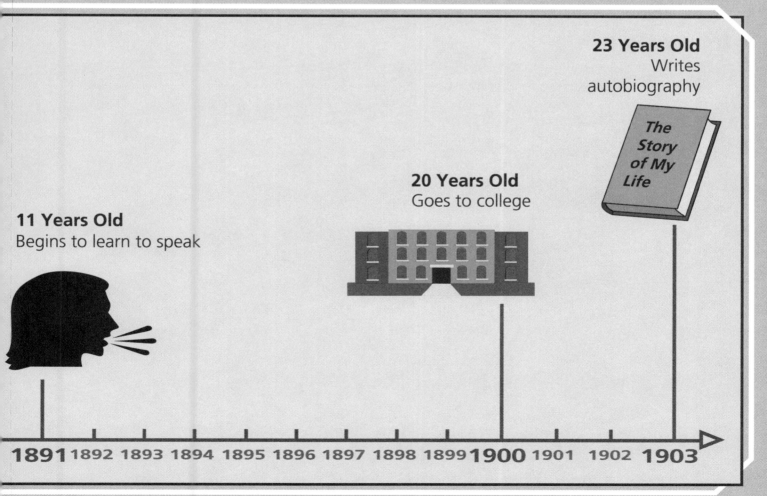

11 Years Old
Begins to learn to speak

20 Years Old
Goes to college

23 Years Old
Writes autobiography

The Story of My Life

1891 1892 1893 1894 1895 1896 1897 1898 1899 1900 1901 1902 1903

Think and Solve

Study the infographic. Answer the questions.

1. Helen Keller began to talk when she was _____ years old.

2. Helen invented Braille.

True   **False**

3. Helen grew up to be a famous _____.

    A. scientist

    B. writer

    C. inventor

    D. teacher

4. The name of Helen's autobiography is _____.

Try It Yourself

Color in the Braille dots to spell the words.

1.

h   a   t

2.

s   t   o   p

3.

b   o   o   k

Make a Time Line

Make a time line of your own life. Write years on the short lines. Start at the bottom with the year you were born. Beside each year, draw and write about important events that happened to you at that time. You do not need to use all the lines.

Your time line should go up to age 23. You'll have to guess about the things that will happen to you between now and then!

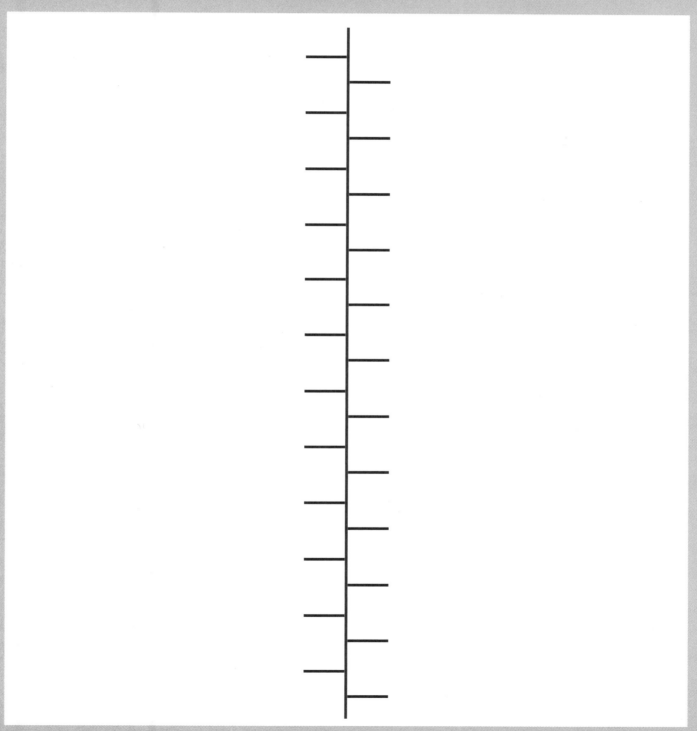

Show Me the Money

Do you get an allowance? Some kids do and some kids do not.
When you get money, you can choose to save it, spend it,
or share it with others. What would you do with an allowance?

Of the kids who get an allowance,
most get between $6 and $10 each week.

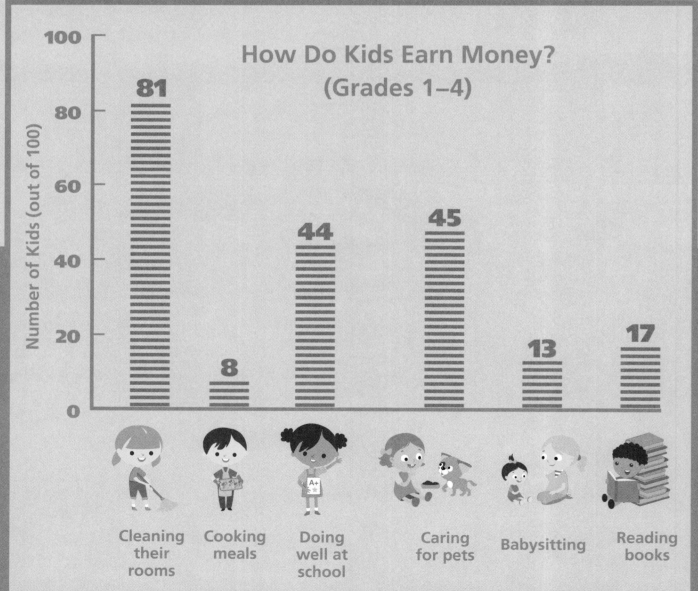

How Do Kids Spend Their Money?

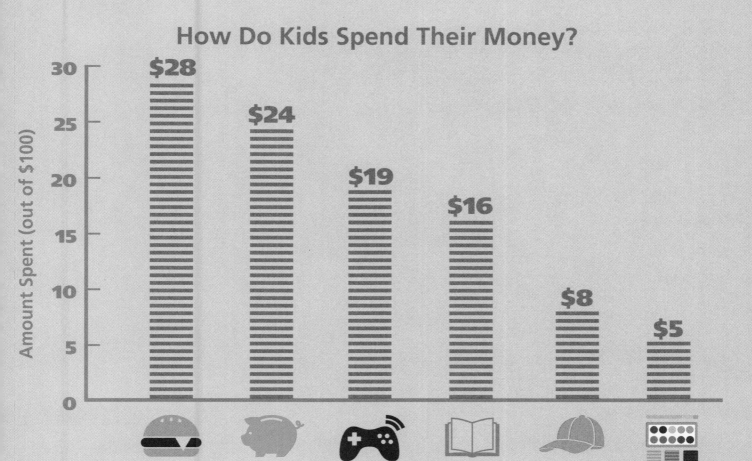

Amount Spent (out of $100)

$28	$24	$19	$16	$8	$5
Food	Savings	Toys and Games	Books and Magazines	Clothes	Other

About **1** out of **3** kids gets an allowance.

Saving 25¢
each day will add up to almost $100 in just one year!

Think and Solve

Study the infographic. Answer the questions.

1. All kids receive some kind of allowance.

True   **False**

2. What do kids spend most of their allowance on?

 A. games

 B. food

 C. clothes

 D. savings

3. Most weekly allowances are between $_____ and $_____ .

Do the Math

Look at each group of bills and coins. Write the total on the line.

1.

$_____. _____ _____

2.

$_____. _____ _____

3.

$_____. _____ _____

Piece It Together

The bills and coins on this page total $10. Imagine this is your allowance. How will you spend it? Cut out the bills, coins, and items with prices. On page 157, glue or tape three items you want to buy. Next to each one, glue or tape the bills and coins you would use to buy it.

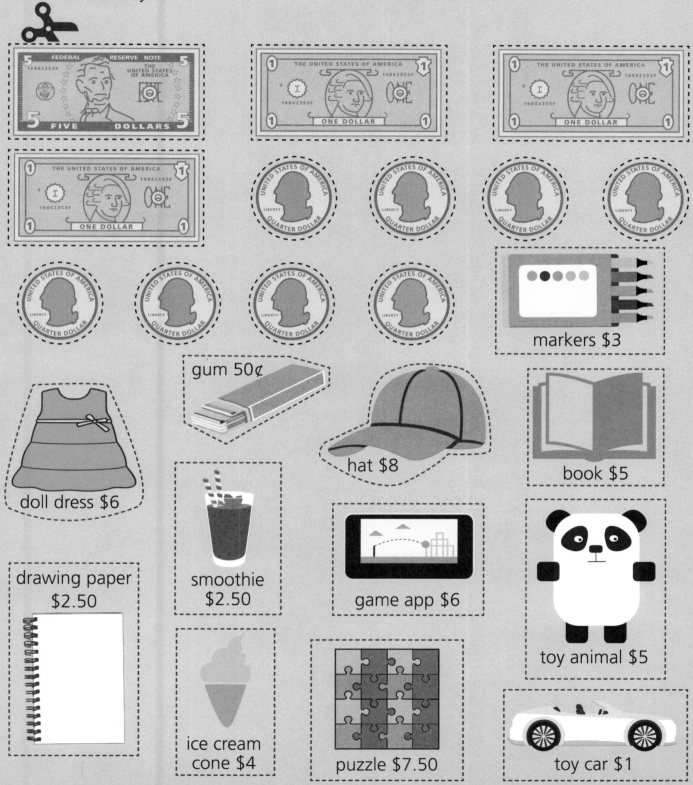

markers $3

gum 50¢

hat $8

book $5

doll dress $6

drawing paper $2.50

smoothie $2.50

game app $6

toy animal $5

ice cream cone $4

puzzle $7.50

toy car $1

Spending My Allowance

What I will buy	How much I need to buy it

Who Needs Bees?

Out of every **100** bee colonies, **30** die each winter.

Bees visit flowers.
They gather nectar. The pollen from the flowers sticks to them. They bring the pollen to other flowers. This is how they pollinate plants and help fruits and veggies grow.

**Plant these flowers
to bring bees to your yard:**
clover, bee balm, catmint, poppies, zinnias, cosmos, and sunflowers.

29

71

Out of the **100** food crops we need most, bees pollinate **71**.

Think and Solve

Study the infographic. Answer the questions.

1. How do bees move pollen from flower to flower?
  A. It sticks to them.
  B. They lick it.
  C. They use their antennae to collect it.
  D. They drink it.

2. Bees pollinate many of the crops that humans use.

True   **False**

3. The title of the infographic is *Who Needs Bees?* What do you think the answer is?

_____

Sequence It

Read about how bees make honey. Then, number the steps in order from 1 to 5.

Worker bees gather nectar from flowers. A bee can carry nectar that weighs almost as much as its own body! When their nectar sacs are full, the bees return to the hive. The nectar is passed mouth-to-mouth among the bees. A special process changes the nectar into honey. The workers put the honey in the cells of the honeycomb. They fan it with their wings. Then, they close up the cells to store the sweet honey.

_____ The bees close up the cells.   _____ The bees fan the honey.

_____ The bees return to the hive.   _____ Worker bees gather nectar.

_____ Bees pass the nectar from mouth to mouth.

Checking Out Libraries

Is your public library one of your favorite places? If not, you should check it out. At the library, you can borrow books, movies, and music, use the Internet, and attend fun programs and workshops—all for free!

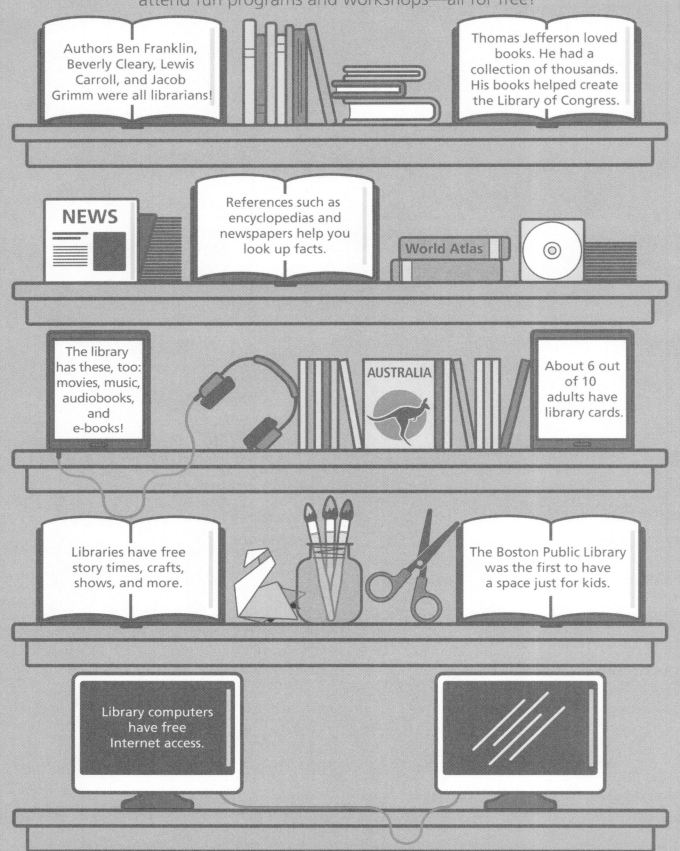

Authors Ben Franklin, Beverly Cleary, Lewis Carroll, and Jacob Grimm were all librarians!

Thomas Jefferson loved books. He had a collection of thousands. His books helped create the Library of Congress.

NEWS

References such as encyclopedias and newspapers help you look up facts.

World Atlas

The library has these, too: movies, music, audiobooks, and e-books!

AUSTRALIA

About 6 out of 10 adults have library cards.

Libraries have free story times, crafts, shows, and more.

The Boston Public Library was the first to have a space just for kids.

Library computers have free Internet access.

12
years to build
the NYPL

1911
the year the NYPL opened

23 million
items in the NYPL

11
feet in length
of the lions that
watch the library

The New York Public Library
(NYPL) is the biggest
public library in the US.

39 inches
height of one of
the NYPL's largest
books (*The Birds
of America*)

THE NEW YORK PUBLIC LIBRARY

1 inch
height of the
smallest book in
the collection

1987
the year that the original stuffed
Winnie-the-Pooh and friends
found a home at the library

125
miles of shelving

Think and Solve

Study the infographic. Answer the questions.

1. The original Winnie-the-Pooh can be found in the New York Public Library.

True   **False**

2. The height of the smallest book in the library is _____ inch.

3. Name one famous author who was a librarian.

_____

4. What president used his book collection to help start the Library of Congress?

_____

Explore Your World

Learn about your public library. Visit the library's website, or visit the library and talk to a children's librarian. Find out four facts about your library. Write them on the cards below.

Make a Plan

Make a plan for books to check out at the library. Check at least five books that you would like to read. Write your own titles on the blank lines.

- [ ] *Miss Nelson Is Missing!* by Harry Allard
- [ ] *Amelia Bedelia* by Peggy Parish
- [ ] *Cloudy With A Chance of Meatballs* by Judi Barrett
- [ ] *Nate the Great* by Marjorie Weinman Sharmat
- [ ] *Are You My Mother?* by P.D. Eastman
- [ ] *Stone Soup* by Marcia Brown
- [ ] *The Day the Crayons Quit* by Drew Daywalt
- [ ] *A Bad Case of Stripes* by David Shannon
- [ ] *Beezus and Ramona* by Beverly Cleary
- [ ] *The True Story of the Three Little Pigs* by Jon Scieszka
- [ ] *Actual Size* by Steve Jenkins
- [ ] *One World, One Day* by Barbara Kerley
- [ ] _____

- [ ] *Castle: How It Works* by David Macaulay
- [ ] *Boy, Were We Wrong About Dinosaurs!* by Kathleen Kudlinski
- [ ] *So You Want to be President?* by Judith St. George
- [ ] *Frogs!* by Elizabeth Carney
- [ ] *How Much Is a Million?* by David M. Schwartz
- [ ] *The Bravest Dog Ever: The True Story of Balto* by Natalie Standiford
- [ ] *Flat Stanley* by Jeff Brown
- [ ] *Mr. Putter & Tabby Pick the Pears* by Cynthia Rylant
- [ ] *Owen* by Kevin Henkes
- [ ] *Sammy the Seal* by Syd Hoff
- [ ] *Rosie Revere, Engineer* by Andrea Beaty
- [ ] *Seeing Symmetry* by Loreen Leedy
- [ ] _____

Celebrate Earth!

Earth Day is like a birthday party for Earth. On this day each year, people around the world give our planet gifts. They do special things to help protect and celebrate the planet we all share.

APRIL						
SUN.	MON.	TUE.	WED.	THURS.	FRI.	SAT.
		1	2	3	4	5
6	7	8	9	10	11	12
13	14	15	16	17	18	19
20	21	22	23	24	25	26
27	28	29	30			

Earth Day

The first Earth Day was held on April 22, 1970. A senator named Gaylord Nelson started it. He wanted a day for people to celebrate our planet. He wanted them to care about keeping it clean and healthy. Today, more than 180 countries celebrate Earth Day.

Keep these words in mind. They will give you ideas for helping Earth all year long!

save green recycle wildlife
trees reuse
walk protect
Earth
clean air climate
carpool animals respect bikes
garden
oceans nature conserve
global organic

How to Go Green on Earth Day

1. Walk or bike to school.

2. Plant a tree.

3. See if you can have a day with no garbage. Reuse or recycle everything.

4. Go to the park or on a walk. Wear gloves and pick up trash you find.

5. Talk to your teacher. Plan a clean-up day for your class at a park.

6. Make posters about helping Earth. Put them up in your school.

7. Turn off the lights when you leave a room.

8. Turn off the water when you brush your teeth.

9. Bring your own bag when you shop.

10. Take short showers.

Think and Solve

Study the infographic. Answer the questions.

1. On what day is Earth Day celebrated?

_____

2. Earth Day was started about _____ years ago.

    A. 10

    B. 25

    C. 50

    D. 100

3. Earth Day is celebrated only in the US and Canada.

    True   **False**

Puzzle It

Read the words about Earth Day. Circle each word in the puzzle.

T	M	O	R	G	A	N	I	C	W	
R	S	K	W	S	D	B	Q	L	P	
E	U	C	X	D	E	O	N	E	I	
E	Q	C	R	R	V	I	R	A	K	
S	V	W	U	E	H	O	D	N	G	
O	D	T	E	C	U	V	G	H	R	
Y	A	G	V	A	B	S	G	B	E	
N	G	J	G	A	R	D	E	N	E	
D	Y	X	E	B	S	T	R	B	N	
C	W	P	J	K	S	O	H	J	S	

trees

Earth

green

garden

clean

organic

nature

reuse

Set a Goal

From the list below, choose one habit you can practice to help Earth. Make a check mark beside it and write it on the line above the chart. Then, try to practice the habit all week long. Use the chart to keep track of your goal. Each day, make a check mark in a box whenever you practice the habit you chose.

☐ Walk or ride your bike to get somewhere.

☐ Reuse or recycle something.

☐ Turn off lights.

☐ Use only a little water to brush your teeth, take a bath or shower, rinse dishes, or do other chores.

☐ Pick up litter (be sure to wear gloves).

☐ Take care of plants and animals.

What I will do for one week: _____

_____

Day 1									
Day 2									
Day 3									
Day 4									
Day 5									
Day 6									
Day 7									

Teddy's Bear

President Teddy Roosevelt went on a hunting trip in 1902. He wanted to see a bear. After three days, there were no bears.

The group he was with wanted to find a bear for him. They wounded a bear. They waited for the president.

The president would not harm the bear. He felt bad for it. This made news. A cartoon was made. It showed Teddy with his back to the bear.

A candy shop owner and his wife had an idea. They put two toy bears in the shop's window. They called them "Teddy's bears."

The "teddy bear" was born!

They sent the first bear to Teddy's children. They asked if they could make more. The president said okay.

Think and Solve

Study the infographic. Answer the questions.

1. The first teddy bear was given to President Roosevelt's children.

True   **False**

2. Teddy Roosevelt was president about _____ years ago.

    A. 10

    B. 50

    C. 100

    D. 200

3. What did President Roosevelt want to see on the hunting trip?

_____

Draw and Write

Tell your own story about an animal. In the first box, draw the beginning of your story. In the second box, draw what happens in the middle. In the third box, draw what happens at the end of your story. Write your story on the lines.

Beginning	Middle	End

_____

_____

_____

The Heart of a Nation

Washington, DC, is not a state. Even so, it is one of the most important parts of the US. How did it become our nation's capital?

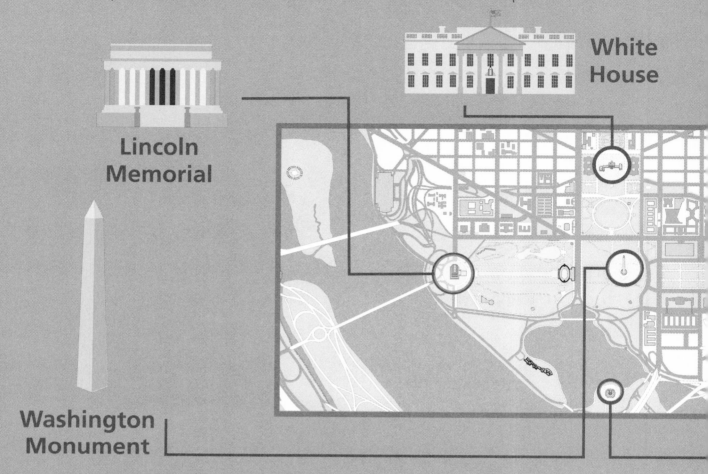

Lincoln Memorial

White House

Washington Monument

Philadelphia was the nation's first capital (from 1790–1800).

Washington chose the new spot for the capital. He chose a French architect to plan the city.

Washington died. The capital was moved to its new city. It was named in honor of George Washington.

John Adams was the first president to live in Washington, DC.

1790

1791

1799

1800

US Capitol

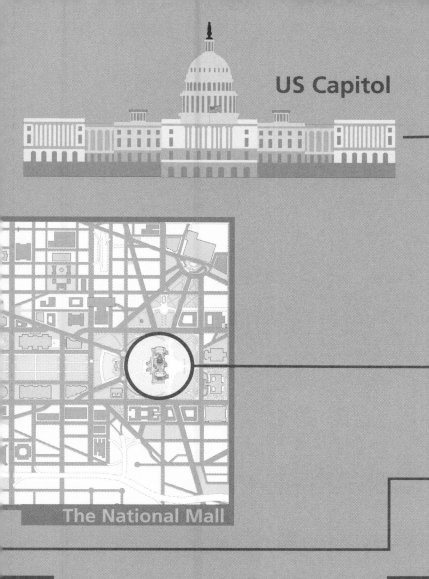

The National Mall

Did you know?
Washington, DC, is smaller than any US state.

MARYLAND

WASHINGTON, DC

VIRGINIA

Jefferson Memorial

The flag of Washington, DC

The design is from George Washington's family.

The British captured and burned Washington, DC, in the War of 1812. Even the White House was burned.

1814

Think and Solve

Study the infographic. Answer the questions.

1. _____ was the first president to live in Washington, DC.

2. Name two famous buildings along the National Mall.

_____   _____

3. Describe the flag of Washington, DC.

_____

_____

Route It

Imagine you are taking a tour of Washington, DC. Look at the schedule below.
On the map, trace the route you might take.

9:00 A.M.—the US Capitol   10:00 A.M.—the White House

12:00 P.M.—the Washington Monument   1:00 P.M.—the Lincoln Memorial

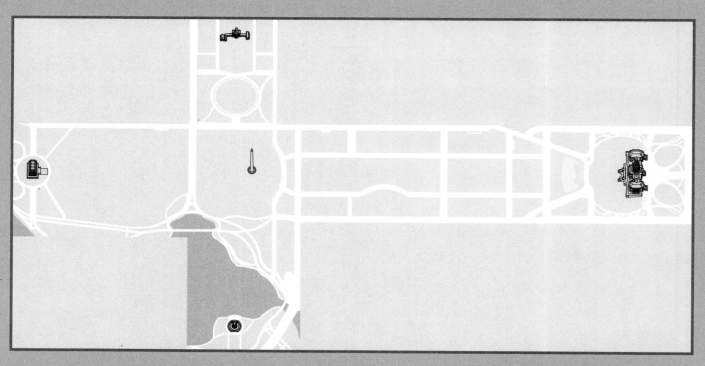

Map It

A *landmark* is a special place in a community that visitors want to see. A landmark can be a park or a natural area, a building, a statue, a fountain, or another place. What landmarks are found in your community? In the space below, draw a map of special places in your town or city. Use the key to help you. Add to the key if you need to.

Landmarks in My Community

Key

 statue, mural, or artwork   hospital

 park or natural area   library

 lake or river   post office

 church or temple   police or fire station

 school   other: _____

 museum   other: _____

The Reason for the Seasons

Why is it cold in winter? Why is it hot in summer? The reason is Earth's tilt.
Earth is tilted as it moves around the Sun.

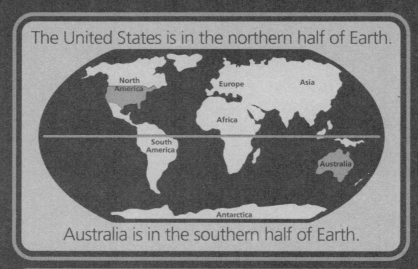

The United States is in the northern half of Earth.

Australia is in the southern half of Earth.

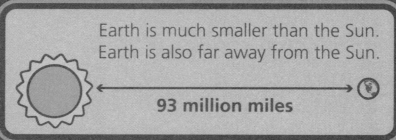

Earth is much smaller than the Sun.
Earth is also far away from the Sun.

93 million miles

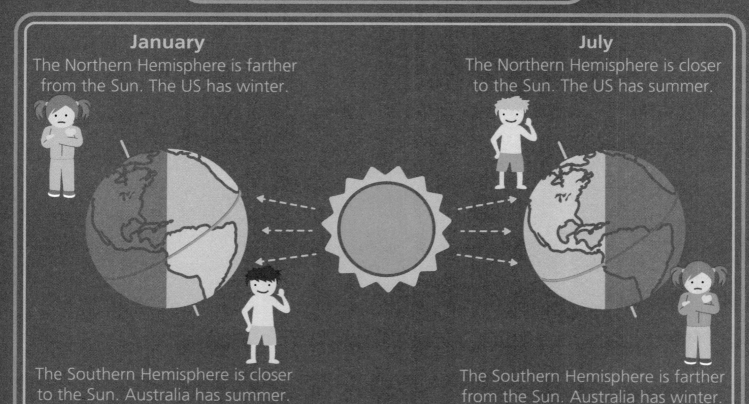

January
The Northern Hemisphere is farther from the Sun. The US has winter.

July
The Northern Hemisphere is closer to the Sun. The US has summer.

The Southern Hemisphere is closer to the Sun. Australia has summer.

The Southern Hemisphere is farther from the Sun. Australia has winter.

Think and Solve

Study the infographic. Answer the questions.

1. When it is winter in the United States, it is winter in Australia, too.

True   **False**

2. The United States is in the (northern, southern) half of Earth. _____

3. Earth is about _____ million miles away from the Sun.

Try It Yourself

Make a model of Earth during different seasons of the year. Follow the directions.

What you need:
- a globe
- a flashlight

What you do:

1. Set the globe on a table. Tilt the North Pole away from you.
2. Shine the flashlight at Earth. The light is the Sun's warmth.

Which half of Earth is closer to the Sun's warmth?   **northern half**   **southern half**
Which half of Earth is having summer?   **northern half**   **southern half**

3. Six months later, Earth is on the other side of the Sun. Tilt the globe so that the South Pole is away from you.
4. Shine the flashlight at Earth.

Which half of Earth is closer to the Sun's warmth?   **northern half**   **southern half**
Which half of Earth is having summer?   **northern half**   **southern half**

A Word From Our Sponsor

Ads are everywhere. They are on TV and the Internet. They are on buses, billboards, and buildings. Sometimes, they are even in schools. What do you think when you see an ad? The person who made it hopes you will want what it is selling.

**Does this ad tell the truth?
Does it tell lies? What do you think?**

This is true. How much is 20 grams of sugar? It is about the same as **7 sugar cubes!**

Only 20 grams of sugar in each serving!

SUPER OATS!

The name is big, bright, and colorful.

Basketball star Nathan Brightly loves them!

**Kids love them!
Moms love them!**

This man is paid to say he likes the cereal.

These kids are actors. They are paid to smile in the photo.

SUPER OATS!

Start your morning right with a bowl of Super Oats! They give your body energy. They give your taste buds a treat!

$15,000,000,000
About 15 BILLION dollars are spent each year on ads for kids!

2,500
Most kids spend about 2,500 hours a year looking at screens: TVs, computers, and phones!

40,000
Most kids will see about 40,000 ads on TV each year!

Think and Solve

Study the infographic. Answer the questions.

1. Does the basketball star really love to eat Super Oats?

   A. no

   B. yes

   C. maybe

   D. The ad does not say.

2. Read each statement. Write *O* if it is an opinion. Write *F* if it is a fact.

   _____ Each serving has 20 grams of sugar.

   _____ The kids in the ad are actors.

   _____ Super Oats give your taste buds a treat.

   _____ Most kids see 40,000 ads in a year.

3. Most kids spend more than 2,000 hours each year looking at screens.

   True   **False**

Explore Your World

The words below are often used in ads. For several days, look and listen for these words. When you see or hear a word in an ad, underline it. You may underline some words more than once.

NEW	save	love	best	healthy
free	quick	MAGIC	easy	SALE
fun	better	taste	great	most

Which word did you see or hear most often? _____

Draw and Write

Pay attention to the ads you see and hear for several days. Then, choose four ads to write about. On each TV screen, draw the ad or commercial. Below the drawing, write what the ad wanted you to do.

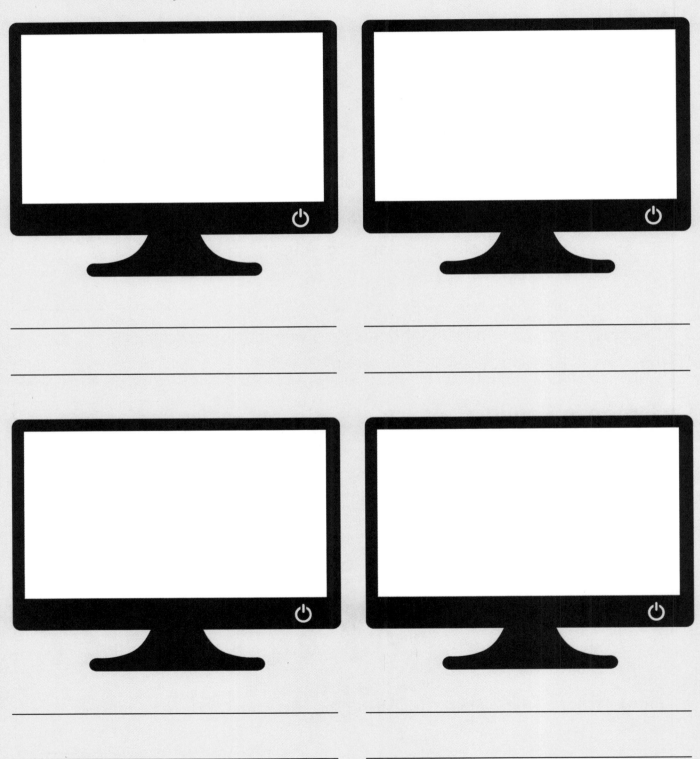

Answer Key

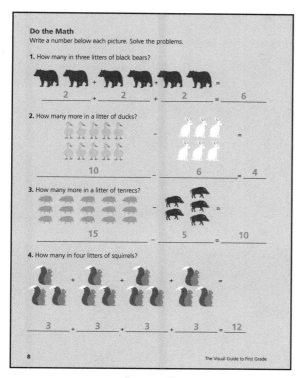

Page 8

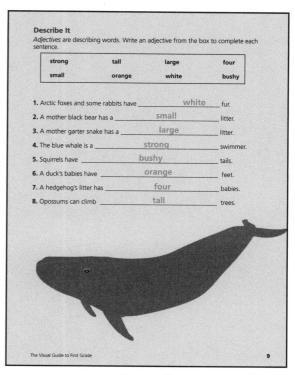

Page 9

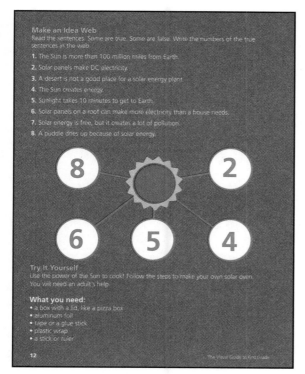

Page 12

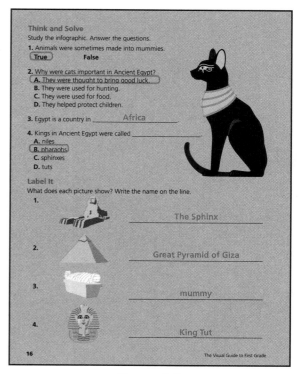

Page 16

Page 21

Think and Solve
Study the infographic. Answer the questions.

1. Write a check mark on the line if the words describe both frogs and toads.

_____ green skin   _____ have long legs

_____ bumpy skin   ____✓_____ hatch as tadpoles

____✓_____ lay eggs   ____✓_____ eat insects

2. All toads are frogs.
(True)   False

3. A _____ toad _____ walks most of the time.

Read About It: Frog or Toad?

SPLASH! LONG LEGS KICK. A smooth body swims. A green head pokes up from the water. Big eyes watch a buzzing bug go by. Zip! A quick tongue shoots out. The insect is gone.

Who ate the bug? Circle your answer.
a toad   (**a frog**)

The Visual Guide to First Grade   21

Page 24

Think and Solve
Study the infographic. Answer the questions.

1. The first cars used steam for power.
(True)   False

2. Gas cost ____20____ cents a gallon in 1920.

3. What came before the first car radio?
A. the first traffic signal
B. the first VW Beetle
C. most cars have seat belts
D. the first drive-through

Label It
Read each statement. Write the year in which the person might have said it. Use the infographic to help you.

My gallon of gas costs 90 cents. ____1979____

I want to drive an SUV. ____1997____

My horseless carriage is electric. ____1884____

I bought a Model T for $850. ____1908____

This new seat belt will keep me safe. ____1965____

24   The Visual Guide to First Grade

Page 28

Think and Solve
Study the infographic. Answer the questions.

1. Most bikes are made _____
A. in the US
B. by the Dutch
(**C.** in China)
D. in Japan

2. The seat of a bike is called a *saddle*.
(True)   False

3. There are about one ____billion____ bikes in the world.

Do the Math
Solve the problems. Use the infographic to help you.

1. Out of 100 trips, how many more do the Dutch make on bicycles than Italians?
____25____ trips

2. How many bikes can fit into two parking spaces for cars?
____30____ bikes

3. Japan makes 5 million bikes each year. India makes 11 million bikes each year. How many more bikes does India make each year?
____6____ million

28   The Visual Guide to First Grade

Page 29

Label It
The prefix *uni-* means "one."   The prefix *bi-* means "two."
The prefix *tri-* means "three."   The word part *cycle* means "circle."

Label each picture with a word from the box.

| tricycle | unicycle | motorcycle | bicycle |

unicycle   motorcycle

bicycle   tricycle

Puzzle It
Look for the names of bike parts in the puzzle. Circle each word.

```
I K N W T F X P N G D G
R O G A S E M A R F N N
X O B M A C K J S I B Q
T I R E D L K C A T E Q
C N O C D A M H O B E D
S W K U L D C R K H Z M
S H S M E E A W C J S X
D B Z S V P H R Z I F Y
F W I S X E A L F D F J
Z E F G E X H U F K U M
T G H L B W G F W B H O
L U W W R Y K Q S C F P
```

tire
wheel
saddle
frame
stem
shock
pedal
chain

The Visual Guide to First Grade   29

Page 32

Study the infographic. Answer the questions.

1. The planet ___Venus___ looks like a bright star.

2. Shooting stars are stars that move quickly across the sky.
True   (False)

3. A rainbow that happens at night is called a ___moonbow___.

4. What are clouds made of?
___drops of water___

Color It
Read each fact. If it tells about something in the day, color the windows blue. If it tells about something in the night, color the windows yellow.

Bats hunt bugs.

Stars are easier to see in the country.

Rainbows happen when light hits raindrops.

Hot-air balloons float.

The Sun gives Earth life.

The ISS can be seen from Earth.

32   The Visual Guide to First Grade

Page 32

Page 35

Mateo's Day

morning   7:00   8:00

afternoon   12:00   3:00

evening   6:00   7:00

night   8:00   9:00

The Visual Guide to First Grade   35

Page 35

Page 38

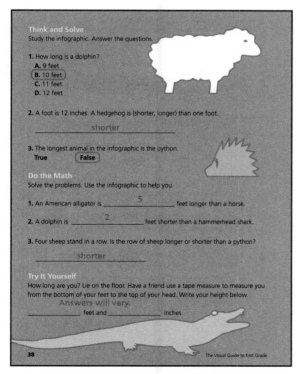

Think and Solve
Study the infographic. Answer the questions.

1. How long is a dolphin?
A. 9 feet
(B. 10 feet)
C. 11 feet
D. 12 feet

2. A foot is 12 inches. A hedgehog is (shorter, longer) than one foot.
___shorter___

3. The longest animal in the infographic is the python.
True   (False)

Do the Math
Solve the problems. Use the infographic to help you.

1. An American alligator is ___5___ feet longer than a horse.

2. A dolphin is ___2___ feet shorter than a hammerhead shark.

3. Four sheep stand in a row. Is the row of sheep longer or shorter than a python?
___shorter___

Try It Yourself
How long are you? Lie on the floor. Have a friend use a tape measure to measure you from the bottom of your feet to the top of your head. Write your height below.
___Answers will vary.___
___ feet and ___ inches

38   The Visual Guide to First Grade

Page 38

Page 42

Think and Solve
Study the infographic. Answer the questions.

1. Which type of home has the same shape as an igloo?
A. tepee
(B. wickiup)
C. longhouse
D. pueblo

2. Pueblos were used by people in the ___Southwest___ part of the US.

3. Which two types of houses were used in the Northeast?
___wickiup___ and ___longhouse___

Match It
Draw a line to match each home with its description.

Wattle and Daub Hut — built by the Navajo

Hogan — up to 400 feet long

Longhouse — also called a *wigwam*

Wickiup — roof made of grass

42   The Visual Guide to First Grade

Page 42

Page 43

Check what was used to make each house. The first one is done for you.

Type of House	grass	mud	brick	wood	animal skins	snow
(house)	✓	✓		✓		
Longhouse				✓		
Wickiup	✓			✓		
Igloo						✓
Hogan	✓	✓				
Tepee				✓	✓	
Adobe Pueblo			✓			

Write About It
Which house would you like to live in? Why?

Answers will vary.

Page 46

Think and Solve
Study the infographic. Answer the questions.

1. Healthy topsoil is mostly water.
   True   (False)

2. In which layers do roots grow?
   A. O and A
   B. B and C
   (C.) A and B
   D. A and C

3. A mole digs tunnels underground. It is looking for insects to eat. Which soil layer does the mole dig in?

   Layer A, topsoil

4. Layer R is the lowest layer. It is called *bedrock*. Tell what you think Layer R is like.

   Answers will vary, but should describe Layer R as being solid rock.

Identify It
Read each statement. Write the letter of the soil layer that is being described.

   B   This layer has the roots of big trees.

   O   This layer has lots of bugs and grass.

   C   This layer has no living things.

   A   This layer is where seeds grow.

Page 49

Going Underground

Layer 0 — Grass — Dead Leaves

Layer A — Worms — Small Roots — Water — Bacteria

Layer B — Big Roots

Layer C — Big Rocks

Layer R — Solid Rock

Page 51

Think and Solve
Study the infographic. Answer the questions.

1. Most presidents were state governors before becoming president.
   True   (False)

The White House

2. A person becomes the new president about one month after being elected.
   True   (False)

3. Which is not a requirement for becoming president?
   A. You must be at least 35 years old.
   B. You must be born a US citizen.
   (C. You must serve in the US Congress.)
   D. You must have lived in the US for at least 14 years.

4. Read about each person. Circle *Yes* if he or she can become president.
   Circle *No* if he or she cannot become president.

   Mia is 55 years old. She was born in Miami, Florida. She has lived in the US her whole life.
   (Yes)   No

   Jonas is 64 years old. He was born in London, England. He came to the US when he was 14 years old. He became a US citizen when he was 22 years old.
   Yes   (No)

   Nancy is 37 years old. She was born in Japan, but she was a US citizen when she was born. She moved back to the US when she was 20.
   (Yes)   No

Page 54

Study the infographic. Answer the questions.

1. Why do you think some animals gain weight before they hibernate?
_____ Answers will vary. _____

2. Squirrels sleep a lot in winter, but they do not hibernate.
(True) False

3. Why do snakes sometimes come out of their burrows in winter?
A. to eat
(B. to get warm)
C. to exercise
D. to get fresh air

Identify It
Write the name of an animal to answer each question.

1. Who sleeps in the mud of a pond? _____ frog or turtle _____

2. Who sleeps inside a tree trunk? _____ bat _____

3. Who wakes up to eat every few days? _____ chipmunk _____

4. Who gains a lot of weight before sleeping? _____ bear _____

5. Who is an insect that hibernates? _____ queen bee _____

54   The Visual Guide to First Grade

Page 55

Read About It:
The Poorwill and the Ladybug

THE POORWILL IS AN UNUSUAL BIRD. It is one of the only birds to hibernate! The poorwill eats insects. When the weather is too cold for insects to live, the poorwill has no food. It will find a hollow log or a patch of grass to sleep in. When the weather gets warm again, the poorwill wakes up.

Another unusual hibernator is the ladybug. In winter, ladybugs huddle together in huge groups. Being together helps them to stay warm. They gather by the hundreds under leaves or bark.

Show It
It is winter in the forest. Draw a poorwill hibernating. Draw a group of ladybugs keeping warm.

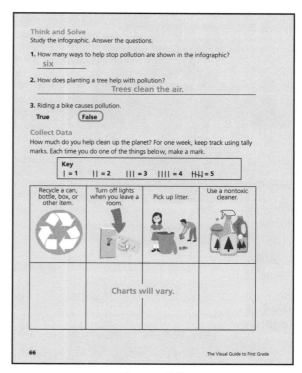

The Visual Guide to First Grade   55

Page 58

Think and Solve
Study the infographic. Answer the questions.

1. Jackie Joyner-Kersee won medals at _____ 4 _____ different Summer Olympics.

2. How many Olympic medals did Jackie Joyner-Kersee win?
_____ 3 _____ gold medals _____ 1 _____ silver medals _____ 2 _____ bronze medals

3. Jackie holds the world record for the highest score in the heptathlon.
(True) False

4. Jackie Joyner-Kersee has _____
A. diabetes
(B. asthma)
C. arthritis
D. hearing loss

Match It
Draw a line from each heptathlon event to its description.

high jump over a bar
100-meter race with jumping
200-meter race
throwing a heavy metal ball
jumping far
throwing a long spear
800-meter race

58   The Visual Guide to First Grade

Page 66

Think and Solve
Study the infographic. Answer the questions.

1. How many ways to help stop pollution are shown in the infographic?
_____ six _____

2. How does planting a tree help with pollution?
_____ Trees clean the air. _____

3. Riding a bike causes pollution.
True (False)

Collect Data
How much do you help clean up the planet? For one week, keep track using tally marks. Each time you do one of the things below, make a mark.

Key
I = 1   II = 2   III = 3   IIII = 4   HHJ = 5

Recycle a can, bottle, box, or other item.	Turn off lights when you leave a room.	Pick up litter.	Use a nontoxic cleaner.
		Charts will vary.	

66   The Visual Guide to First Grade

The Visual Guide to First Grade

Page 69

Study the infographic. Answer the questions.

1. There are more elephants in Africa than any other animal.

True   (False)

2. Which animal has the smallest population?

__dama gazelle__

3. The northern part of Africa is mostly (forest, desert).

__desert__

4. Write the population for each animal.

Gorilla ___4,500___   Lion ___20,000___

Hyena ___10,000___   Chimpanzee ___150,000___

Make a Chart

For each animal, draw an X in the chart to show where it lives. Some animals will need more than one X.

	Lion	Elephant	Dama Gazelle	Hyena	Chimpanzee
Desert			X		
Grassland	X	X		X	
Forest	X	X		X	X

Page 72

Study the infographic. Answer the questions.

1. Some petroglyphs show patterns instead of pictures.

(True)   False

2. There are more petroglyphs in __North America__ than anywhere else.

3. The oldest petroglyphs are more than _____ years old.
   A. 2,000,000
   B. 200,000
   (C.) 20,000
   D. 2,000

4. Why do you think ancient people made petroglyphs?

__Answers will vary.__

Read About It: Petroglyphs

Study the petroglyphs and their meanings. You will use them to make a story on the next page.

Page 76

Study the infographic. Answer the questions.

1. The Moon looks ___red___ during a total lunar eclipse.

2. When the Moon makes a shadow on Earth, it is called a _____.
   A. full moon
   B. lunar eclipse
   (C.) solar eclipse
   D. partial lunar eclipse

3. You should never look directly at the Sun.

(True)   False

Do the Math

The dates in the chart show when total solar eclipses and total lunar eclipses will happen. How old will you be for each one? Write your answers in the chart.

Total Eclipses	
Date	Your Age
July 2, 2019 (solar)	Answers will vary.
May 26, 2021 (lunar)	Answers will vary.
November 8, 2022 (lunar)	Answers will vary.
April 8, 2024 (solar)	Answers will vary.

Page 80

Study the infographic. Answer the questions.

1. How many mammals are shown in the infographic?

__three__

2. Which animal jumps farther than a record-breaking human athlete?

__kangaroo__

3. A snow leopard can jump as far as 50 feet. Where would a snow leopard appear in the infographic?

__after the kangaroo__

Do the Math

Solve the problems. Use the infographic to help you.

1. A grasshopper can jump more than _____ feet.
   (Hint: 1 foot = 12 inches)
   (A. 3)
   B. 13
   C. 36
   D. 48

2. A tree frog jumps two times.
   How many feet does it jump in all?

   ___14___ feet

3. How much farther can a kangaroo jump than a mountain goat?

   ___28___ feet

4. A mountain goat jumps three times. How many feet does it jump in all?

   ___36___ feet

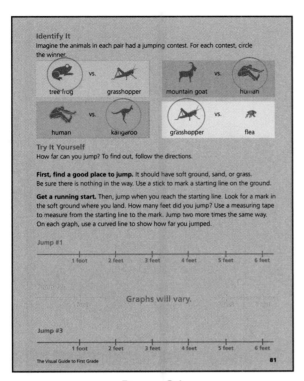

Page 81

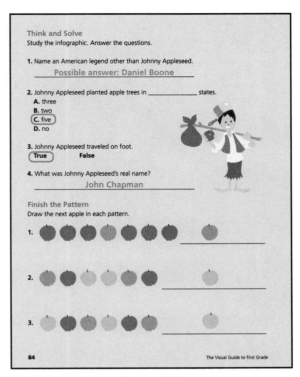

Page 84

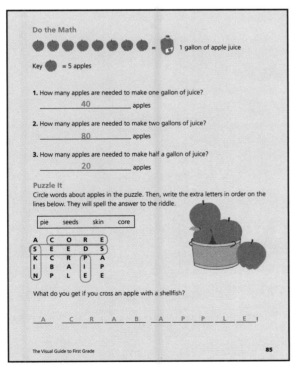

Page 85

Page 88

Page 89

The web shows how many teeth different types of animals have.
Use it to answer the questions below.

How Many Teeth?

anteater: **0**
dog: **42**
mouse: **16**
cat: **30**
pig: **44**
goat: **32**
black bear: **42**
lion: **30**

1. Which animal pairs have the same number of teeth?
   __black bear__ and __dog__
   __cat__ and __lion__

2. A pig has ____2____ more teeth than a black bear.

3. Two goats together have ____64____ teeth.

4. A lion has ____30____ more teeth than an anteater.

5. Number the animals below in order, from least to most teeth.
   __4__ pigs   __2__ cats   __3__ dogs   __1__ mice

Page 89

Page 96

Study the infographic. Answer the questions.

1. If the wind is blowing at 20 mph, what would it measure
   on the Beaufort Wind Scale?
   ____5____

2. What happens when hot air rises?
   __Cool air takes its place.__

3. In what order are the hurricanes listed in the infographic?
   A. alphabetical
   B. the years when they happened
   C. how strong the winds were
   D. how long the hurricane lasted

4. Wind is moving air.
   True   False

Explore Your World
Can you see wind? No, but you can see what it does. Go outside and look for the
wind. Circle the signs of wind you see.

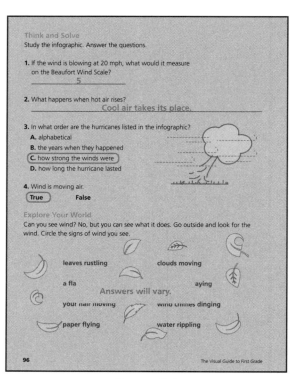

leaves rustling   clouds moving

a fla   aying

__Answers will vary.__

your hair moving   wind chimes dinging

paper flying   water rippling

Page 96

Page 102

Study the infographic. Answer the questions.

1. A scorpion's tail has ____six____ parts.

2. Most scorpions are deadly to humans.
   True   False

3. Scorpions live on all continents except _____
   A. North America
   B. Antarctica
   C. Australia
   D. Europe

4. What does it mean to say that scorpions are *nocturnal*?
   __They sleep during the day and are active at night.__

Solve the problems. Use the infographic to help you.

1. How many legs do two scorpions have?
   16

2. The largest type of scorpion is eight inches long. How much shorter is this than
   one foot? (Hint: 1 foot = 12 inches)
   ____4____ inches

3. A scorpion, a spider, and a ladybug have _____ legs altogether.
   A. 16
   B. 20
   C. 22
   D. 28

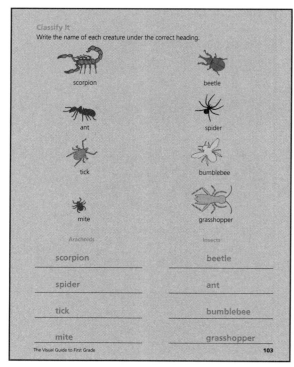

Page 102

Page 103

Write the name of each creature under the correct heading.

scorpion   beetle
ant   spider
tick   bumblebee
mite   grasshopper

Arachnids	Insects
scorpion	beetle
spider	ant
tick	bumblebee
mite	grasshopper

Page 103

Page 105

Think and Solve
Study the infographic. Answer the questions.

1. Libraries did not exist 100 years ago.
True **(False)**

2. You want to know today how much an elephant weighs. Where could you find the answer?
_____ Possible answer: on a computer/Internet _____

3. Imagine you are living 200 years ago. You want to know how to bake bread. How do you find the answer?
_____ Possible answer: Ask an adult. _____

Match It
Draw a line to match each question to the best place to find the answer.

How many tablespoons are in one cup?

What countries border France?

What does the word *stubborn* mean?

What year did my grandparents come to America?

Page 105

Page 108

Think and Solve
Study the infographic. Answer the questions.

1. A cotton gin separates the ____cotton____ from the ____seed____.

2. What is a loom used for?
A. to clean cotton
(B. to make cloth)
C. to dye shirts
D. to cut cloth

3. One T-shirt has about six miles of yarn in it.
(True) False

4. The steps needed to make a shirt are shown below. Number them in order from 1 to 8.

7	Sew	1	Harvest
3	Spin	5	Finish
4	Knit	8	Cut
2	Gin	8	Dye

5. What happens when the cloth is washed?
A. The cloth turns gray and rough.
B. The cotton separates from the seed.
(C. It becomes softer.)
D. The cloth is folded and cut.

Page 108

Page 112

Think and Solve
Study the infographic. Answer the questions.

1. Write one example for each type of animal.
carnivore: Possible answer: bobcat
herbivore: Possible answer: white-tailed deer
omnivore: Possible answer: raccoon

2. How many insects are shown in the infographic?
3

3. Bats are the only nocturnal animals that fly.
True **(False)**

4. Why do toads often sit under lights?
to catch bugs that fly around the light

Match It
Look at the footprints. Match each set of footprints to the animal that made them.

deer

toad

owl

raccoon

bobcat

Page 112

Page 116

Do the Math
Solve the problems. Use the infographic to help you.

1. There are three bananas in each bunch. How many are there in four bunches?
____12____ bananas

2. Three monkeys climbed a tree. Six more monkeys joined them.
How many monkeys were in the tree? ____9____ monkeys

3. A monkey grabbed 12 bunches of bananas. It dropped three bunches.
How many bunches were left? ____9____ bunches

4. About how many pounds of bananas do two Americans eat in one year?
____54____

Page 116

Page 117

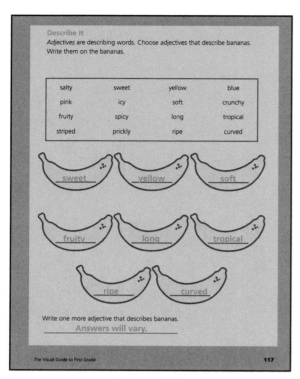

Describe It

Adjectives are describing words. Choose adjectives that describe bananas. Write them on the bananas.

salty	sweet	yellow	blue
pink	icy	soft	crunchy
fruity	spicy	long	tropical
striped	prickly	ripe	curved

sweet   yellow   soft

fruity   long   tropical

ripe   curved

Write one more adjective that describes bananas.
Answers will vary.

Page 120

Think and Solve
Study the infographic. Answer the questions.

1. Most wildfires are not caused by humans.
   True   (False)

2. Which is not a way to fight wildfires?
   A. aircraft
   (B. arson)
   C. firebreaks
   D. controlled burns

3. Which type of wildfire burns along treetops?
   crown fires

4. On the map, which state has more acres burned than any other?
   A. Washington
   (B. Oregon)
   C. Florida
   D. Texas

Write About It
Think of a solution for each problem. Write your ideas in the chart.

Problem	Solution
People throw out lit cigarettes near woods.	Solutions will vary.
People do not put campfires out all the way.	Solutions will vary.
People burn garbage. The fires can get out of control.	Solutions will vary.

Page 121

Identify It
Look at the picture. Circle five things that could start a wildfire.

Page 123

Think and Solve
Study the infographic. Answer the questions.

1. How does a giraffe's height help it?
   The giraffe can spot danger. It can reach leaves high in trees.

2. An adult female giraffe is ___10___ feet taller than a human man.

3. Wild giraffes are found in every part of Africa.
   True   (False)

Explore Your World
What is longer than a giraffe's tongue? What is shorter than a giraffe's tongue? Use a string to find out.

Use a ruler or a tape measure to measure 21 inches on a string. Ask an adult to help you cut the string so it is 21 inches long. Then, use your string to measure things inside and outside. Find four things that are longer than a giraffe's tongue. Find four things that are shorter than a giraffe's tongue. Write the name of each thing in the chart under the correct heading.

Shorter than a giraffe's tongue	Longer than a giraffe's tongue
Charts will vary.	

Page 117

Page 120

Page 121

Page 123

Page 126

Think and Solve
Study the infographic. Answer the questions.

1. What is a bucket brigade?
   a line of people passing along buckets of water

2. Early firefighters often had to walk to fires.
   (True)   False

3. What do modern fire trucks have that early steam pumpers did not?
   A. a pump
   B. wheels
   C. a driver
   (D. a siren)

Classify It
Read the list of equipment. Write *E* if it was used by early firefighters.
Write *T* if it is used by firefighters today.

1. __T__ plastic helmet
2. __E__ horses
3. __T__ siren
4. __E__ wool clothing
5. __E__ leather hoses
6. __E__ bucket brigade
7. __T__ light, protective clothes
8. __T__ plastic hoses

Page 126

Ready to Fight Fires!

Page 129

Page 132

Think and Solve
Study the infographic. Answer the questions.

1. Are there more fireplaces or bathrooms in the White House?
   bathrooms

2. Which president did not live at the White House?
   George Washington

3. What is the name of the street where the president lives?
   Pennsylvania Avenue

4. The president lives at the White House, but works in another building.
   True   (False)

Match It
Draw a line from each room to the sentence that tells about it.

The Rose Garden — It holds maps from around the world.

The China Room — It is the president's office.

The Oval Office — It is where dishes are displayed.

The Map Room — It is filled with flowers.

Page 132

Page 136

Think and Solve
Study the infographic. Answer the questions.

1. Where is Mammoth Cave?
   (A. Kentucky)
   B. South Dakota
   C. New Mexico
   D. Texas

2. Stalagmites grow up from the floor of a cave.
   (True)   False

3. How much longer is Jewel Cave than Wind Cave?
   __37__ miles

4. Two caves are almost the same length. Which caves are they?
   __Wind__ Cave and __Lechuguilla__ Cave

Puzzle It
Find words about caves in the puzzle. Circle them.

| cave | bats | stream | crystal | crab | spelunk |

```
B  D  S  C  R  A  B
V  N  P  A  J  P  C
G  L  E  H  O  R  R
U  O  L  I  C  E  Y
F  Q  U  B  A  T  S
P  N  N  M  V  S  T
F  S  K  X  E  Z  A
S  T  R  E  A  M  L
```

Page 136

Page 139

Stalactites

2 feet · 4 feet · 7 feet · 12 feet · 16 feet · 21 feet · 29 feet

---

Page 141

Think and Solve
Study the infographic. Answer the questions.

1. The US grows more soybeans than any other country except China.

   True   (False)

2. List three ways soybeans are used as food.

   _____ Answers will vary. _____

3. List three ways soybeans are used other than as food.

   _____ Answers will vary. _____

4. What is the top crop grown in the US?

   _____ corn _____

Explore Your World
Take a look at food products in your kitchen. Which foods have soy in them? Read the list of ingredients on each food package closely. Look for the word *soy*. Try to find at least five foods that have soy as an ingredient. List them below.

_____ Lists will vary. _____

_____ _____

Page 146

Think and Solve
Study the infographic. Answer the questions.

1. Which type of star is closest to Earth?
   A. an orange giant
   B. a red supergiant
   C. a yellow dwarf
   D. a white supergiant

2. A white dwarf star is _____
   A. a very hot, small star
   B. a cool, very large star
   C. a very hot, very large star
   D. a very cool, small star

3. The brightest star in Earth's southern skies is *Polaris*.
   True   (False)

4. Supergiants last the longest time because they have the most fuel.
   True   (False)

Sequence It
Number the stars from 1 to 6. Use 1 for the hottest star and 6 for the coolest star.

  4   2   5   3   1   6

Page 150

Think and Solve
Study the infographic. Answer the questions.

1. Helen Keller began to talk when she was _____ 11 _____ years old.

2. Helen invented Braille.
   True   (False)

3. Helen grew up to be a famous _____
   A. scientist
   B. writer
   C. inventor
   D. teacher

4. The name of Helen's autobiography is The Story of My Life .

Try It Yourself
Color in the Braille dots to spell the words.

1.   h   a   t

2.   s   t   o   p

3.   b   o   o   k

Page 139

Page 141

Page 146

Page 150

Page 154

Study the infographic. Answer the questions.

1. All kids receive some kind of allowance.
True   (False)

2. What do kids spend most of their allowance on?
A. games
(B. food)
C. clothes
D. savings

3. Most weekly allowances are between $_____6_____ and $_____10_____.

Do the Math
Look at each group of bills and coins. Write the total on the line.

1. $_____6___.___5___8___

2. $_____3___.___5___1___

3. $_____1___.___9___2___

154   The Visual Guide to First Grade

Page 159

Think and Solve
Study the infographic. Answer the questions.

1. How do bees move pollen from flower to flower?
(A. It sticks to them.)
B. They lick it.
C. They use their antennae to collect it.
D. They drink it.

2. Bees pollinate many of the crops that humans use.
(True)   False

3. The title of the infographic is *Who Needs Bees?* What do you think the answer is?
_____Answers will vary._____

Sequence It
Read about how bees make honey. Then, number the steps in order from 1 to 5.

Worker bees gather nectar from flowers. A bee can carry nectar that weighs almost as much as its own body! When their nectar sacs are full, the bees return to the hive. The nectar is passed mouth-to-mouth among the bees. A special process changes the nectar into honey. The workers put the honey in the cells of the honeycomb. They fan it with their wings. Then, they close up the cells to store the sweet honey.

___5___ The bees close up the cells.   ___4___ The bees fan the honey.

___2___ The bees return to the hive.   ___1___ Worker bees gather nectar.

___3___ Bees pass the nectar from mouth to mouth.

The Visual Guide to First Grade   159

Page 162

Think and Solve
Study the infographic. Answer the questions.

1. The original Winnie-the-Pooh can be found in the New York Public Library.
(True)   False

2. The height of the smallest book in the library is _____one_____ inch.

3. Name one famous author who was a librarian.
_____Possible answer: Beverly Cleary_____

4. What president used his book collection to help start the Library of Congress?
_____Thomas Jefferson_____

Explore Your World
Learn about your public library. Visit the library's website, or visit the library and talk to a children's librarian. Find out four facts about your library. Write them on the cards below.

📖 **Library Card**
Library facts will vary.

📖 **Library Card**
Library facts will vary.

📖 **Library Card**
Library facts will vary.

📖 **Library Card**
Library facts will vary.

162   The Visual Guide to First Grade

Page 166

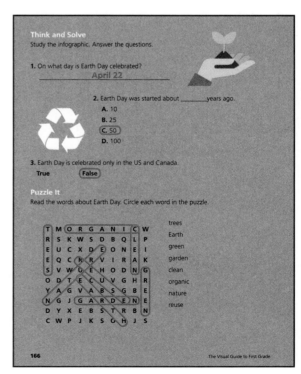

Think and Solve
Study the infographic. Answer the questions.

1. On what day is Earth Day celebrated?
_____April 22_____

2. Earth Day was started about _____years ago.
A. 10
B. 25
(C. 50)
D. 100

3. Earth Day is celebrated only in the US and Canada.
True   (False)

Puzzle It
Read the words about Earth Day. Circle each word in the puzzle.

```
T M O R G A N I C W        trees
R S K W S D B Q L P        Earth
E U C X D E O N E I        green
E Q C K R V I R A K        garden
S V W U E H O D N G        clean
O D T E C U V G H R        organic
Y A G V A B S G B E        nature
N G J G A R D E N N        reuse
D Y X E B S T R B N
C W P J K S G H J S
```

166   The Visual Guide to First Grade

Page 169

Study the infographic. Answer the questions.

1. The first teddy bear was given to President Roosevelt's children.
(True)   False

2. Teddy Roosevelt was president about _____ years ago.
A. 10
B. 50
(C. 100)
D. 200

3. What did President Roosevelt want to see on the hunting trip?
_____ a bear _____

Draw and Write
Tell your own story about an animal. In the first box, draw the beginning of your story. In the second box, draw what happens in the middle. In the third box, draw what happens at the end of your story. Write your story on the lines.

Beginning	Middle	End
	Drawings and stories will vary.	

_____

_____

_____

Page 172

Study the infographic. Answer the questions.

1. __John Adams__ was the first president to live in Washington, DC.

2. Name two famous buildings along the National Mall.
_____ Answers will vary. _____

3. Describe the flag of Washington, DC.
It has a white background, three red stars at the top and two red stripes.

Route It
Imagine you are taking a tour of Washington, DC. Look at the schedule below. On the map, trace the route you might take.

9:00 A.M.—the US Capitol   10:00 A.M.—the White House
12:00 P.M.—the Washington Monument   1:00 P.M.—the Lincoln Memorial

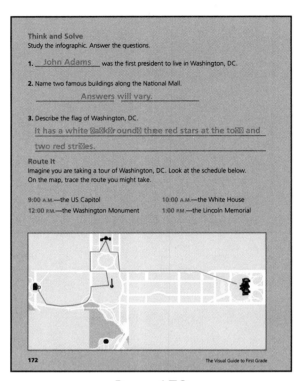

Page 175

Study the infographic. Answer the questions.

1. When it is winter in the United States, it is winter in Australia, too.
True   (False)

2. The United States is in the (northern, southern) half of Earth. __northern__

3. Earth is about __93__ million miles away from the Sun.

Try It Yourself
Make a model of Earth during different seasons of the year. Follow the directions.

What you need:
• a globe
• a flashlight

What you do:
1. Set the globe on a table. Tilt the North Pole away from you.
2. Shine the flashlight at Earth. The light is the Sun's warmth.

Which half of Earth is closer to the Sun's warmth?   northern half (southern half)
Which half of Earth is having summer?   northern half (southern half)

3. Six months later, Earth is on the other side of the Sun. Tilt the globe so that the South Pole is away from you.
4. Shine the flashlight at Earth.

Which half of Earth is closer to the Sun's warmth?   (northern half) southern half
Which half of Earth is having summer?   (northern half) southern half

Page 177

Study the infographic. Answer the questions.

1. Does the basketball star really love to eat Super Oats?
A. no
B. yes
(C. maybe)
D. The ad does not say.

2. Read each statement. Write O if it is an opinion. Write F if it is a fact.
___F___ Each serving has 20 grams of sugar.
___F___ The kids in the ad are actors.
___O___ Super Oats give your taste buds a treat.
___F___ Most kids see 40,000 ads in a year.

3. Most kids spend more than 2,000 hours each year looking at screens.
(True)   False

Explore Your World
The words below are often used in ads. For several days, look and listen for these words. When you see or hear a word in an ad, underline it. You may underline some words more than once.

Answers will vary.

NEW	save	love	best	healthy
free	quick	MAGIC	easy	SALE
fun	better	taste	great	most

Which word did you see or hear most often? _____